Living & Working in New Zealand

Living & Working in New Zealand

How to build a new life
in New Zealand

JOY MUIRHEAD
5th edition

howtobooks

Cover images by kind permission of Tourism New Zealand.

Published by How To Books Ltd,
3 Newtec Place, Magdalen Road,
Oxford OX4 1RE. United Kingdom.
Tel: (01865) 793806. Fax: (01865) 248780.
e-mail: info@howtobooks.co.uk
http://www.howtobooks.co.uk

First published 1994
Second edition 1994
Third edition 1996
Fourth edition (revised) 1997
Fifth edition (revised) 2001
Reprinted 2002

British Library Cataloguing in Publication Data
A catalogue record for this book is available from
the British Library

Cover design by Baseline Arts Ltd., Oxford

Produced for How To Books by Deer Park Productions
Typeset by PDQ Typesetting, Newcastle-under-Lyme, Staffs.
Printed and bound by The Cromwell Press, Trowbridge,
Wiltshire

NOTE: The material contained in this book is set out in good
faith for general guidance and no liability can be accepted
for loss or expense incurred as a result of relying in particular
circumstances on statements made in the book. Laws and
regulations are complex and liable to change, and readers should
check the current position with the relevant authorities before
making personal arrangements.

Contents

List of Illustrations

Preface
to the fifth edition

Congratulations, you must have discovered that New Zealand is not just another part of Australia!

My husband and I brought our three children here in 1972. We had no friends or relations to come to: we just decided that it would be a good place in which to bring up our family. The only information we had received from New Zealand House in London was that we should buy a house in New Zealand before we arrived! We decided that was certainly not a good idea.

After poring over maps of New Zealand, we came to the conclusion that the North Island was going to be sub-tropical, and therefore we wouldn't need our warm English clothes, and told the children to take their last look at the pleasure of open fires, because we just would never see one again. This proved to be wrong; only north of Auckland in the Bay of Islands area does one find truly sub-tropical weather. As we settled in the Bay of Plenty, we found it very hot in summer, but when the temperature dropped to around 10 degrees Celsius after summer highs of 25–30 degrees Celsius, we certainly felt it cool enough to light a fire.

New Zealand lived up to the clean green image we had, the skies were certainly blue and the waters clear, and the sun was so bright we needed sunglasses to cut down the glare.

One day we were travelling from Hamilton in the North Island to Tauranga, a journey of perhaps one hour. After about 20 minutes I realised that there were no cars to be seen, and what's more, there were no people either! It felt as though a bomb had been dropped and we were the only people alive – a strange feeling. However, it now seems strange to meet many cars when on the open road; you only meet congestion and experience hold-ups when travelling through the cities.

The children got teased about their 'pommie accents' and it took a while for them to settle in at school and make friends, but that was in 1972 and there is a lot more tolerance these days towards new immigrants.

I hope that this book, based on more than 23 years' first-hand experience, will be of some help to you in planning your stay in New Zealand – and who knows? – perhaps making a whole new life here as so many have before. It is pleasing to see such great interest in New Zealand, making it necessary for a fifth edition of this book. This new edition has been revised and updated to reflect the latest information for visitors and new residents.

Finally, I would like to express my thanks to the following organisations for giving so much valuable help and advice during the preparation of this book:

Ambler Collins, immigration and commercial consultants
NZ Immigration Service
NZ Police Department
KPMG Peat Marwick, Wellington office
Ministry of Education
Department of Statistics
New Zealand Medical Association
NZ Employment Service

Joy Muirhead

Fig. 1. Map of New Zealand.

1

Making the Big Decision

Aotearoa – The Land of the Long White Cloud
Kia-Ora – this is the traditional Maori welcome.

INTRODUCING THE COUNTRY

We have established that New Zealand is not just another part of Australia. It is also as far away from England as you can go without finding yourself on the way back again! It is 1,600 kilometres east of Australia and it consists of two major islands, the North Island and the South Island, plus a number of smaller islands, with a total land area of 270,500 square kilometres. It has a population of approximately 3.8 million people and 46 million sheep, that is about 12 sheep per head of population!

The islands of New Zealand have been ethnically and culturally connected to Polynesia for at least 1,000 years. Less than 200 years ago, its population and cultural heritage was wholly that of Polynesia, but now New Zealand is dominated by cultural traditions that are mainly European, emanating especially from Great Britain.

Some four-fifths of New Zealanders are of European origin, predominantly from the British Isles, but also including people from the Netherlands, former Yugoslavia, Germany and other nations. The indigenous Maori population make up the next largest group of the population, about 9.6%. The third main ethnic group is the Pacific Island Polynesians who make up about 6%.

New Zealand has a high standard of education and its qualifications are recognised internationally. Professor Marie Clay from Auckland University is well known for her remedial reading observations and recommendations.

The birds and the bees

One of the main factors in influencing me to make New Zealand my home was the fact that there are hardly any creepy crawlies here!

There are no snakes or crocodiles. We do have one spider which is poisonous – the Katipo. I have never seen one although I do know that they can sometimes be found in decaying logs, so I just stay away from dead wood!

Twenty years ago there were no wasps here but there are now. We get mosquitos, especially in the north of the North Island, and there are flies, but not in the horrendous numbers they have in Australia. Yes, we do have sharks in our waters and there have been a few attacks on swimmers.

First impressions

When you first arrive you will be enchanted by the gaily painted houses, which are mainly of wooden construction with tin roofs. You will be surprised at the spaciousness of everything, and even on a busy day on Queen Street, Auckland, you can still walk in reasonable comfort. You may notice the seemingly small selection of goods in the shops, and possibly be told, when enquiring for something, that they are waiting for the next shipment!

Bare knees

New Zealand lifestyle is very casual. Shorts and shirts for the men and sundresses for the women are the norm during the summer. I found it strange to see butchers wearing shorts, knee socks and an apron! When I went to see the doctor, I had to try not to smile when he came around from his desk as he too was wearing shorts!

QUESTIONS AND ANSWERS

Does the water really go down the plughole in the opposite direction?

Yes, it does, all due to the earth's rotation and the fact that New Zealand is in the Antipodes.

Is sheep the only meat available in New Zealand?

No, even though sheep do outnumber people 12 to 1!

Is New Zealand sub-tropical?

In the north of the North Island it is.

Do the women wear grass skirts?
Definitely no! The women are very fashion conscious.

Has New Zealand ever been a penal colony?

No, but we have our fair share of criminals.

Do the trees grow twice as fast as anywhere else?

Yes, certain species do, because the growth doesn't stop during the winter.

THE ATTRACTIONS OF NEW ZEALAND

What are you looking for?

- A smaller population?
- A better climate?
- Long stretches of white sandy beaches?
- Clear blue skies?
- Freedom from terrorism?
- Nuclear free country?

Yes, you will find all these here, and there are still good opportunities for hard-working people who are adaptable to new lifestyles and traditions.

The beaches, especially from the Bay of Plenty in the North Island northwards, are spectacular with clean white sand and clear blue sea – you could be forgiven for thinking you were on a desert island. But the summers can be hot and dangerous. New Zealand now has the highest incidence of skin cancer in the world. We are constantly being reminded of the 'burntime' each day, and children in schools wear sun hats and everyone is urged to 'cover up' in the sun. Protective sun creams are essential. So think of these very real dangers if the climate is the main reason for your intended move.

John Burnett and his wife and family came to New Zealand from Surrey, England in the late 1960s. John and his wife were both school teachers. They bought their own home and soon acquired two cars and a boat for weekend pleasure trips. When the children left home John and his wife bought a new home with a view of the Pacific Ocean, and now they lead a much to be admired lifestyle.

Peter Spencer and his wife Joan and two boys arrived in New Zealand in 1989; Peter was an engineer. They were able to buy some land and start building their own home, but before it was finished they were so homesick for England they sold up and went back to Birmingham.

Jim and Sheila Murray-Hamilton came to New Zealand from England in 1990. They have set up a very successful fashion business in Wellington and say they love New Zealand because there is still a lot to offer here. Jim grew up in Scotland and Sheila grew up in Wolverhampton, England.

A non-nuclear region
In 1987 the New Zealand Government, at the time being the Labour Party led by David Lange, informed the American Government that we would no longer allow nuclear-powered ships in our waters, and this is still the case. New Zealand is proud to be a nuclear-free country, and after the Chernobyl type disasters this makes New Zealand appear a very attractive haven.

A pollution-free land?
Not quite: we do have water pollution. In the Hauraki Gulf, which is around the Auckland area, swimmers have been warned not to swim in certain areas because of pollution. Some parts of the Bay of Plenty, also in the North Island, have been declared unfit for swimmers, due to some degree of farm pollution pouring into the inner Tauranga Harbour.

Air pollution is also a problem in the Christchurch area, which is in the South Island. This is caused by open fires in the winter which create horrendous smogs which exceed the international safety standards.

In 1993 a natural phenomenon occurred which caused a type of pollution to our shellfish industry. An algae bloom caused a toxin infection to bivalves which are shellfish with two shells ie scallops, oysters and mussels. When the toxin disappeared, and the shellfish had been washed clean by several clear tidal flows, they were inspected and declared fit for human consumption once more. However, some areas are still affected but they are expected to clear naturally given time. Any shellfish for sale now are perfectly safe to eat, having first been cleared by the authorities.

CLIMATE

Weather varieties
The climate varies from sub-tropical in the far north to the almost continental in the mountainous areas of the South Island. However because of the oceanic surroundings the climate is not extreme.

There are of course always the exceptions. In 1991 there were three major floods and the worst affected regions were Westland and Otago in the South Island, and Wairarapa in the North Island.

The Westland flood was the worst in 30 years, and many people had to be evacuated from their homes. The total rainfall for January 1991 was the highest in 125 years. In the Wairarapa heavy rain caused severe flooding during 8–11 March when two rivers burst their banks. Stock losses were severe.

Greenhouse gases

New Zealand with its large forested areas, low population and hydro-electric power generation, was believed to be a carbon dioxide sink, but testing has revealed that New Zealand is a net producer. This production has been associated with the high consumption of fossil fuels and gradual deforestation. New Zealand's emissions of carbon dioxide are twice the world average per capita.

We also have higher than average methane emissions; eight times the world average per capita. Most sources of methane have been identified, but there is still debate about how much can be attributed to each separate source. Amazingly enough most is produced by micro-organisms working in the guts of such animals as sheep and cattle and with 46 million sheep alone, that is a lot of gas!

Earthquakes and volcanic eruptions

The level of seismic activity in New Zealand is moderate compared with other countries lying in the almost continuous belt of earthquake activity around the rim of the Pacific. A shock of Richter magnitude 6 or above happens on average about once a year, and a shock of magnitude 7 or above once in ten years, with a shock of magnitude 8 perhaps once a century.

There were two earthquakes of magnitude 6 or greater in 1990 and six exceeding 5.5. And in 1991 there were two earthquakes exceeding magnitude 6. The largest one in September was felt from the top of the North Island to the middle of the South Island.

In September 1995 Mt Ruapehu, in the centre of the North Island, erupted sending spectacular lava flows which ran like black streaks down the snow clad mountain, disrupting the winter ski season. In June 1996 another spectacular fireworks display occurred, once again spoiling the ski season momentarily – the ash clouds disrupted air traffic across the centre of the North Island and carried inches of dust across the vineyards of Hawkes Bay.

Avalanches

We also get freak cold snaps, and in 1991 the Shotover River near Queenstown in the South Island froze over for the first time in a hundred years. Heavy snow also contributed to frequent avalanches on major ski fields and caused loss of life on Mount Ruapehu in the North Island. The Milford road in the South Island was closed for two weeks 6–20 August due to an avalanche risk.

Tornadoes

Occasionally we experience tornadoes, and sometimes there is building damage and people get injured. On 14 April 1991 a band of thunderstorms passed over Auckland in the North Island leaving behind a trail of damage, and a man was critically hurt. Tornadoes were also seen in the Bay of Plenty on 30 April 1991. I actually saw a garage roof lifted and blown across the road.

The seasons

Spring	September to November
Summer	December to February
Autumn	March to May
Winter	June to August

SOME BRIEF FACTS

Latitude	33° to 53° south
Longitude	162° to 173° west
Total area	26.9 million hectares
Farms	14.4 million hectares
Forest	8.1 million hectares
National parks	2.3 million hectares
Highest mountain	Mount Cook, South Island, 3,764m
Population	3.8 million (North Island, 2.8 million) (South Island 1 million) (approx)
Capital	Wellington, South Island

MULTICULTURALISM

Population

According to recent Department of Statistics figures, out of a total population of 3.8 million people, approximately 75% are New Zealand European, 10% New Zealand Maori, 6% Pacific Island

Polynesian, 1.5% Chinese, 2% Asian, 1% Indian. (These groups do not total 100%. Some people are counted in two or more ethnic groups.)

Latest population growth figures
Statistics New Zealand stated recently that New Zealand's population grew from 3,781,300 in the year to December 1997 to 3,803,900 by 1998, an increase of 22,600. The average age was approximately 33.9 years compared with 33.6 in 1997.

Maori
The majority of Maori live in the north of the North Island, from Hamilton and the Bay of Plenty northwards. Today there is no true Maori, as intermarriage has diluted the race.

The modern Maori is well represented in the workforce, particularly in Government departments. The Maori people are represented by the Ministry of Maori Affairs which was formed on 1 July 1989. This Ministry provides a Maori perspective in policy making.

There are five Maori seats in Parliament, and as a result of the MMP (Multi Member Representation) voting system, Maori are now represented in a number of other electorates.

The language
The number of native speakers of Maori has been declining over the last hundred years in the face of strong competition from English, but in recent decades there has been a renewal of interest in the language on the part of the **Kohanga Reo** (Maori Language Pre-School Movement) and more recently the **Kura Kaupapa Maori** (Maori Language Immersion Primary Schools).

Many Maori radio programmes have now been established as well as Maori television programmes.

The Maori Queen
1991 marked the 25th anniversary of the coronation of Te Arikinui Dame Te Atairangikaahu as the Maori Queen and leader of the Kingitangi movement. She is the first woman to head the movement. Te Atairangikaahu belongs to the Waikato Confederation of Tribes and is a direct descendent of the famous Waikato leader Te Puea Herangi.

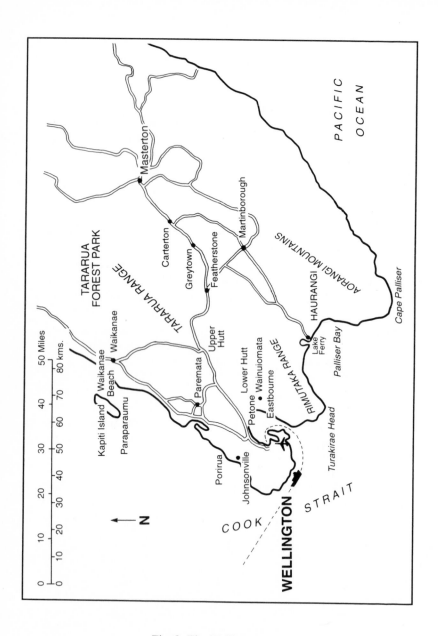

Fig. 2. The Wellington area.

Maori legends
Maori legends abound, and one in particular tells of the formation of the North Island. Maui is said to have fished up the North Island of New Zealand – Te Ika a Maui – from his great canoe, the South Island. Maui and his brothers struggled with a large fish, beating and slashing it so that it writhed in agony creating the hills and valleys. When the fish died it became a great land where previously there had been nothing but the ocean.

The southern part of the North Island is said to be the head of the fish – Te upoko a te Ika. Wellington Harbour is the mouth of the fish – Te Waha o te Ika, and Lake Wairarapa the eye of the fish – Te Whatu o te Ika.

When the fish was hauled up, the mouth formed a lake separated from the sea by a barrier of land. This lake trapped two taniwha – sea monsters – named Ngake and Whaitaitai. Ngake didn't like being trapped so he smashed his way through to the open sea. The wreckage he left created the entrance to the harbour.

Whaitaitai decided he would go out to sea as well, but on the way he got stuck in the shallow water as the tide went out. He remained there for two centuries, being revived by the tide washing in and out and preventing him from drying out.

In 1460 there was a great earthquake and Whaitaitai was uplifted and died, becoming the present day Miramar Peninsula. His soul, or wairua, left him in the form of a bird called Te keo and flew to a nearby hill and wept. The hill was thus called 'Tangi te keo' although the European name for it is Mt Victoria.

NEW ZEALAND'S MAIN CITIES

Wellington

Wellington is the capital of New Zealand, and it is nestled at the southern end of the North Island. It appears to be sprouting out from the creases of the many hills, like a plant searching for a hold. It has been the capital of New Zealand since 1865. It has a fine deep harbour which is said to be one of the most picturesque in the world. The population totals approximately 329,000.

Wellington is renowned as being the 'Windy City' with gusts of wind over 60 kilometres per hour. It has an average of 199 windy days per year. The climate fluctuates between 7 degrees Celsius to a high of approximately 23 degrees Celsius. It is also reputed to have one restaurant for every day of the year!

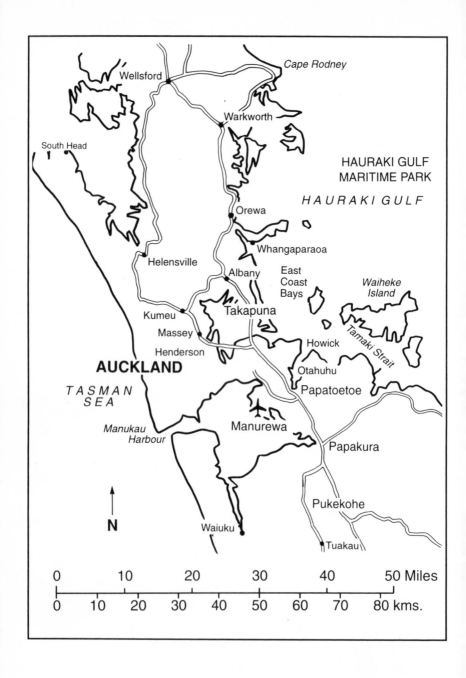

Fig. 3. The Auckland area.

Wellington is the world's most southern capital, and it is the only capital in the 'Roaring Forties' latitude. Nearly all Wellingtonians live within 3km of the sea, and Wellington Airport is the busiest in the South Pacific.

Wellington is the National Headquarters for the National Museum, Art Gallery, National Archives, National Library, New Zealand School of Dance, Royal New Zealand Ballet Company, New Zealand Symphony Orchestra, New Zealand Drama School and Government departments. A splendid new Museum of New Zealand opened in 1998, offering New Zealanders the very latest in technology and presentation.

Separated by Cook Strait, Wellington is the major connecting link with the South Island. You can catch the ferry at the Ferry Terminal, the cost being approximately $59 per adult and $35 per child one way in summer. Cars cost approximately $190 one way.

Auckland

Auckland is the second major city in the North Island, and it is New Zealand's largest urban centre with more than one-quarter of the national total population in a region of 5,580 square kilometres. The population totals 1.3 million. It is the largest Polynesian centre in the world.

Auckland is considered to be the commercial centre of New Zealand, and is also known as 'The City of Sails' because of the huge number of sailing craft moored in and around its waters. It has a superb coastline on each side of this narrow neck of land, with Waitemata Harbour on the east side and the Manukau Harbour on the west. The city's most scenic drive follows a coastal route, with views out to Rangitoto Island, the volcanic cone that is so much a part of Auckland.

The Waitemata Harbour and the Hauraki Gulf have a big influence on Auckland's leisure time. Auckland's Anniversary Day on 27 January brings out yachts for one of the largest one-day Regattas in the world. Auckland will be the venue for the next America's Cup, which will be held on the Hauraki Gulf. The climate is close to sub-tropical but it is classified as a warm temperate which reaches an average of 23 degrees Celsius in the summer and around 15 degrees Celsius in the winter.

Hamilton

Hamilton is New Zealand's largest inland city and fifth largest urban area with a population of 153,800. It is conveniently situated in the centre of the North Island, and is one of the richest pastoral farming regions of the world. Cambridge, which lies on the outskirts of Hamilton and is a 15 minute drive from the city, is world renowned for its horse breeding. Hamilton is a drive of approximately 90 minutes from Auckland. The Waikato River runs through the centre of Hamilton – this is the longest river in New Zealand.

Within a radius of 150 kilometres of Hamilton there are more than 2.3 million people, that is over 60% of New Zealand's total population. It is located on four State Highways and has the biggest railway junction in New Zealand.

There are enormous recreational opportunities within Hamilton and the immediate surroundings. Trout fishing, sailing, wind surfing and water skiing are available on the region's rivers and lakes. World class rowing facilities are available at Lake Karapiro, a 20 minute drive from Hamilton.

Winters can be cold, with an average temperature of 13 degrees Celsius during the day and an occasional low of 0 degrees Celsius during the night. Summer days can be long, warm and sunny, with temperatures around 20 to 25 degrees Celsius. There is abundant rainfall, between 800 and 1,500mm per year. Rain falls throughout the year, with more falling in the winter.

New Plymouth

Around a thousand years ago a giant flightless bird moved through virgin indigenous forests and browsed at the edge of vast flax swamps of a still active volcanic cone. This was the scene discovered in about the 11th century by the first settlers to the Taranaki areas who stalked the large bird for food, called it the **Moa**, and harvested the flax to make clothing.

The Moa is now extinct but its cousin the **Kiwi**, a much smaller flightless bird, still frequents remaining forest areas. Much of the forest was cleared for farming by European settlers who began arriving in the 1840s. Small townships sprang up, the first being New Plymouth, which became a city in 1948 and is the main servicing centre for the province of Taranaki.

New Plymouth is situated on the west coast of the North Island, and is dominated by the majestic Mount Egmont/Taranaki, which stands 2,518m high and is only 32 kilometres south of the city. The life and climate of New Plymouth seems to be dominated by this fabulous mountain, which some days can remain hidden from view by strange large clouds gathered around its peak, and yet the rest of

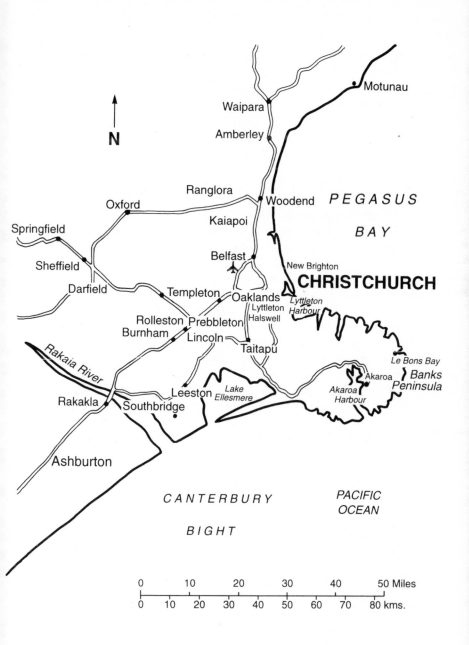

Fig. 4. The Christchurch area.

25

the skies can be clear.

New Plymouth was made affluent by the exploitation of oil and gas reserves. The local oil industry is said to be one of the oldest established in the world. There are lots of attractions for its 68,000 residents in the form of seven golf courses, rivers, lakes and beaches. The summer temperature averages 17–20 degrees Celsius, and in the winter 10 degrees Celsius.

Christchurch

Cathedral City, Garden City of the Plains, English City – the most English city outside England. These are all phrases to describe the capital of Canterbury in the South Island. The Botanic Gardens bordered by the gentle flowing Avon River are said to be among the best in the world.

When English settlers arrived in 1850 on the 'First Four Ships' they began building their city and the English influence is still seen today. It was designed as a model Anglican settlement, a clean geometric grid of a city laid over wild swamp and scrubby plainsland. By the late 1890s the English immigrants had already turned it into a tree studded, neo-gothic recreation of 'home'.

Christchurch is at the centre of New Zealand's third most populous area after Auckland and Wellington, with a population of 318,100. The metropolitan areas sprawl over the Canterbury Plains and lower Northern Plains. It is linked to its seaport at Lyttleton Harbour, 11 kilometres south of the city centre by rail and tunnel. It also has an International Airport, as Christchurch is the gateway to the Southern Alps and Queenstown, which is a very busy tourist attraction. It is also the base for Antarctic expeditions, and it is here that you can get a real taste of the Antarctic by visiting the International Antarctic Centre.

Christchurch is very flat and a very popular form of transport is by bicycle. There are eight skifields to choose from within two hours' drive of the city, including the internationally renowned slopes of Mount Hutt.

Located 43 degrees south of the Equator, Christchurch has an unpredictable climate, with a summer temperature of around 25 degrees and a winter temperature of approximately 9 degrees Celsius, but these temperatures can fluctuate at any time of the year, and it is not unknown for Christchurch to experience a temperature of 20 degrees Celsius in the winter!

Dunedin

Dunedin, capital of the province of Otago, is located at the head of Otago Harbour on the lower east coast of the South Island. It was founded in 1848 by Scottish migrants and is a four hour drive to Christchurch and a comfortable four hour drive to the Alpine resort of Queenstown. It is the second largest urban area in the South Island, after Christchurch, and has a population of around 112,400.

Dunedin is the coldest of the main centres. The summer temperature is around 19 degrees Celsius, and a minimum of 2.5 degrees Celsius in the winter. Its rainfall is spread throughout the year.

Culture mingles side by side with recreation in Dunedin. Amongst the city's parks and playing areas should be mentioned Carisbrook Park, scene of many important cricket and rugby games. The nearby beaches of St Clair and St Kilda attract thousands of bathers in the summer. The southern Lakes District is just three hours' drive away, and from there the inspiring grandeur of Fiordland and South Westland a mere stone's throw away.

Invercargill

Invercargill is the southernmost city in the British Commonwealth. It was founded on the shores of the Waihopai River estuary in 1856. Legendary whaler and farmer Johnny Jones is said to have bought a huge block of land which included Invercargill from the Maori and the price he is said to have paid was 12 muskets and a whaleboat!

The first inhabitant is said to have been John Kelly, an Irishman who saw a business possibility as a boatman ferrying new settlers ashore from the vessels that brought them to New Zealand. Invercargill attracted a large number of Scottish immigrants, and the Scottish street names bear witness to this.

Invercargill is very flat and symmetrically laid out, and has a population of approximately 52,000. It is the capital of the province of Southland. The giant aluminium smelter at Bluff plays a very important part in the economic life of Invercargill. The province also produces wool, wheat, barley, beef and the deer farmed in the area produce velvet. The temperature is approximately 18 degrees Celsius in the summer, with a winter temperature of approximately 7 degrees Celsius.

Minnie Dean

The most infamous character in the history of Invercargill was Minnie Dean. She was Minnie McCulloch and a widow when she arrived in Invercargill in 1868. She was only 21 years of age and she had two daughters from her first marriage. It was said that she was the niece of the first European woman to live in the town.

Within four years she had married Charles Dean. After 14 years they were still childless and her two other daughters had grown up and presumably moved away. They adopted Mary Cameron and bought a house on 20 acres.

Minnie set herself up as a 'baby farmer'. Victorian attitudes meant that unmarried mothers were sinful and babies were hastily given for adoption. Minnie adopted children outright, or kept them until foster homes could be found. At times there were as many as ten children including babies a few months old in the small three-roomed house.

Mary Cameron, her adopted daughter, found work as a dressmaker and was out of the house during the day; her husband also worked during the day. She would tell them that adoptive parents had been found for several of the children, as they left and were replaced by 'new' ones. The truth was, Minnie disposed of some of the children to make room for more. It is said that she killed some of them with laudanum, and buried them in her garden.

The trial was closely followed throughout New Zealand, and particularly in Invercargill. Minnie said that dozens of 'her' children were in foster homes, but she couldn't say where as she had never kept records. Minnie was sentenced to death. She was hanged at 8am on 12 August 1895 protesting her innocence. She was 47 years old.

Minnie Dean was the only woman ever to be hanged in New Zealand.

2

Immigration

MORE MIGRANTS NEEDED

New Zealand welcomes applications from people wishing to come here, whether it is to visit, study, work or live. New Zealand needs people who are 'keen to make a go of it', people with qualifications and experience, who would not be a drain on our resources.

It will cost you money to process your application for residency, and unfortunately if you find that you have not been successful, you will not receive a rebate of the fees you have paid. So it is a good idea to assess your chances before having to 'pay up', by filling in the specimen self assessment form in this chapter. If after having assessed your points you wish to proceed further, go to your nearest immigration office and apply for a residency permit. Remember, you then have to go through *their* assessment. Do *not* make any serious plans to move *until you have received your residency permit*.

There are many New Zealand Immigration Offices around the world where expert help and information can be received, and the necessary application forms applied for. See addresses at the back of this book.

Policy in the temporary field has been aimed to facilitate the entry of tourists and business visitors, and New Zealand has arrangements for visa-free entry for citizens of over 25 countries. See the section on Visitors for a list of these countries.

If, on the other hand, you are not from a visa-waiver country, or if you wish to undertake any of the following:

- you want to study
- you want to work at a job you have already arranged
- you are sponsored for a visit by a relative or friend in New Zealand
- you want to get medical treatment

then you will need to apply for a visa. Three months is the standard period for a visit to New Zealand for visitors from both visa-waiver and visa-required countries.

If you wish to extend your visit, you must demonstrate viable means of support or other good reasons, before a further three month permit will be granted. British citizens only can receive a six months' permit on arrival. You may also apply for a further visitor's permit if there are good reasons why you cannot leave New Zealand, or if you are a genuine tourist.

If you know you want to visit New Zealand for more than three months before you arrive, then you should apply for a visa to stay the length of time you require (up to 12 months) *before* travelling to New Zealand, whether you are from a visa-required or visa-waiver country.

Visitors who do not apply in advance for a longer stay are usually only permitted to be in New Zealand for a stay of up to six months in any 12 month period. You must then leave this country, and stay away for the same period you were here, *eg* if you were here for six months, then you must stay away for six months before turning to New Zealand again as a visitor.

Applications for work permits are considered in the light of the local labour market. Policy allows entry on student visas of people wishing to undertake long-term courses at universities and other tertiary institutions, although some courses of less than three months' duration can be attended without a student permit. Provision is also made for people to enter New Zealand for medical treatment in certain circumstances.

HOT NEWS

A new immigration category will be introduced in March 2002 in the form of a 'Talent Visa'. A 'Skill Shortage' permit is also to be introduced. As these details are still being finalised I urge you to access website http://www.immigration.govt.nz for further information or contact your nearest NZ immigration office.

The categories

Now we come to the 'hard bit' – delving through numerous pages of information on immigration requirements. So that you can pick out the part that is relevant to you we have divided the sections as follows:

- Visitor's permit
- Study permit
- Work permit
- Residency.

OBTAINING A VISITOR'S VISA/PERMIT

Visitors may come to New Zealand:

- as tourists
- for business talks
- to see friends or relatives
- to play sport or perform in cultural events (without pay)
- for medical treatment or medical consultation.

You will definitely need a visitor's visa *before* you travel here unless you are:

- an Australian citizen travelling on an Australian passport (you *do not* need a visa and are exempt from the requirement to hold a permit to be in New Zealand)

- an Australian resident with a current Australian resident return visa (you *do not* need a visa and are granted a residence permit when you arrive)

- a citizen of any of the following countries, which have visa-waiver agreements with New Zealand.

Note: you *must* apply for a visa if you plan to visit for more than the time stated below:

For visits up to 30 days
Citizens of France living in Tahiti or New Caledonia.

For visits up to three months
Citizens of Austria, Belgium, Brunei, Canada, Denmark, Finland, France[1], Germany, Greece, Iceland, Indonesia, Ireland, Italy, Japan, Korea (South), Kiribati, Liechtenstein, Luxembourg, Malaysia, Malta, Monaco, Nauru, Netherlands, Norway, Portugal[2], Singapore, Spain, Sweden, Switzerland, Thailand, Tuvalu, United States of America.

Notes: [1]French citizens living in France only. [2]Portuguese passport holders must have the right to live permanently in Portugal.

For visits up to six months
British citizens and other British passport holders who have evidence of the right to live permanently in the United Kingdom.

If you are a citizen of one of the above stated countries, you can apply for a visitor's permit (see page 33) by completing an arrival card when you arrive in New Zealand.

Visitor's visas

A visitor's visa is an endorsement in your passport *before* you come to New Zealand. You should apply for your visitor's permit when you complete an arrival card upon entering New Zealand. The period of time you are allowed to stay will be written inside your visa and permit, and you are *not* entitled to work in New Zealand. Visas are to enable you to:

- study or train for a single course of not more than three months
- undergo medical treatment
- take a holiday.

You will need to supply a completed **Application for Visitor's Visa**, fee, passport, and a recent passport-size photo. You may also be required to show that you have enough money to support yourself during your stay here, *ie* NZ $1,000 for each person per month or NZ $400 each person per month if your accommodation is already paid, and evidence of this – prepaid hotel vouchers – must be available. Details of your travel arrangements to leave New Zealand must also be shown.

If you wish to make more than one journey to New Zealand, you should apply for a multiple visa.

Medical treatment

If you are coming to New Zealand for medical treatment you may have to give details of treatment by completing a **Details of Intended Medical Treatment** form. You will also need a letter from a New Zealand hospital (Crown Health Enterprise) or Regional Health Authority to your doctor confirming your acceptance for treatment. For private sector treatment, you will need a letter from a New Zealand doctor or hospital confirming that you have been accepted for treatment. Evidence that you will be able to pay for treatment is also required.

Yacht and private aircraft

You will require a visa if you are travelling by private aircraft or yacht, unless you are a citizen of one of the visa-waiver countries listed in this chapter, also if you are only visiting for no longer than the time stated in that section. Application for a visitor's permit is made by completing an arrival card when you land in New Zealand.

What is a visitor's permit?
A visitor's permit is endorsed in your passport. It shows that you have permission to be in New Zealand. The period of time you are allowed to stay here is written on the permit.

You *may not* work here if you have a visitor's permit. It is also illegal for you to study for longer than three months if you have a visitor's permit. If you have a visitor's permit and want to work in New Zealand or to study for longer than three months you must make an application to either change to a work or student permit or change the conditions of your visitor's permit.

You will only be granted permission to work if there are no suitable New Zealand job seekers who could do the job you have been offered. Also, you will only be able to work for the remaining time you are entitled to stay as a visitor.

How do I apply for a visitor's permit?
When you arrive in New Zealand you apply for a visitor's permit by completing an arrival card. You will need to show your passport which must be valid until at least three months past the date you plan to leave New Zealand, and your visitor's visa (if you had to obtain one before you travelled to New Zealand). If you are already in New Zealand you should apply to an office of the New Zealand Immigration Service (see the addresses at the back of this book).

Documents
To make an application you will need to supply:
1. A completed *Application for Visitor's Permit* form.
2. The application fee (see this chapter).
3. Your passport (which must be valid until at least three months past the date you plan to leave New Zealand).
4. A recent passport-sized photo.

Money
You will also be asked to show that you have enough money to support yourself whilst in New Zealand, see this chapter for details, plus evidence of funds which can be in the form of traveller's cheques, bank draft, letters of credit or a New Zealand bank account in your name. Cash or credit cards may be accepted as evidence of funds.

Guarantees

If you do not have enough money you will need a guarantee of accommodation and maintenance from a friend or relative who lives in New Zealand. In this case you must use the form **Sponsoring a Visitor**. In addition you will need to show details of travel arrangements for your departure from New Zealand, such as valid tickets to a country to which you have the right of entry.

How long can I stay?

The length of stay shown in the permit granted on your arrival will depend on whether you entered under a visa-waiver agreement and were able to meet the requirements for a visit of the time specified in the agreement, or you obtained a visitor's visa before you departed for New Zealand.

All visitors to New Zealand are allowed a stay of up to nine months, provided they apply for further permits (if required) and meet normal visitor requirements. You *must* apply for a further permit if you want to extend your stay. A further visitor's permit allowing a stay of more than nine months many only be granted to people who are genuine tourists, or who have lodged a residence application for the first time, and this is being considered, or if you cannot leave New Zealand because of circumstances beyond your control. This permit will be for a period of not more than three months, to a maximum stay of twelve months, from the date of your arrival.

You might also be granted a further visitor's permit if you are undergoing medical treatment or your private yacht or aircraft needs repair. Owners of private craft may be granted further permits beyond the standard maximum stay when their craft needs to undergo refitting or major repairs. You will need to show evidence of this.

Finding a sponsor

If you are applying for a visitor's visa or visitor's permit, but do not have enough money for your living expenses or onward travel, you may be sponsored by a friend or relative in New Zealand.

Such sponsors must be resident in New Zealand and be a New Zealand citizen or have a residence permit *without requirements*, or be exempt from the requirements to hold a permit.

They must be prepared to cover the cost of your maintenance (or living expenses), accommodation and tickets for you to leave New Zealand. Any dependants must also be listed on this form. Your sponsor should complete the form **Sponsoring a Visitor** and take it to an office of the New Zealand Immigration Service in New Zealand for approval. After approval your sponsor should send it to you so that you can attach it to your application for a visitor's visa.

It must be noted that if sponsors fail to carry out their undertaking, the New Zealand Government may recover from them any costs incurred in respect of that failure (this could include the cost of accommodation and tickets for departure if the person has to be removed from New Zealand).

Could I be refused a visa or permit?

Yes, you could if you did not meet the standard requirements for getting a visitor's visa or permit, or if you are not eligible for a permit under Section Seven of the **Immigration Act 1987**. You could be refused entry if:

- you have been convicted and sentenced to prison for five years or more†

- in the past ten years you have been convicted and sentenced to prison for twelve months or more†

- you have been deported from any country

- you are subject to a current New Zealand removal warrant or removal order

- the authorities suspect you of being a terrorist or likely to commit a crime.

† This applies even if your offences have been later taken off the record.

OBTAINING A STUDY VISA/PERMIT

Visas

A visa is an endorsement placed in your passport *before* you depart for New Zealand. Visas allow you to travel to New Zealand until the specified date, they do not give you permission to be in New Zealand, but do indicate that the holder has permission to travel to New Zealand, and that the issuing officer knows of no reason why a permit should not be issued upon arrival. You must apply for a visa *unless* the course of study or training is for three months or less. A visa shows the length of your stay, *eg* up to four years. This will also be shown on your permit.

If you wish to enquire about technical institutions, universities and schools, you can contact either the Ministry of Education, International Division, Private Bag, Wellington, New Zealand, tel: 64-4-473 5544 or fax 64-4-499 1327, or the institution of your choice. The addresses can be found at the back of this book, together with the Immigration Service Offices (NZ addresses) and the New Zealand Ministry of Education offices (see Chapter 4 on education).

Before you apply

There are two courses of action to take *before* applying for a visa:

1. You must have a letter of acceptance for the course of your choice, from the New Zealand institution of your choice. A specimen application form is shown on page 88.

2. You must show that the fees have been paid, by presenting your receipt.

You must then have the following information which must be attached to your application for a visa:

(a) Your passport or certificate of identity. Your passport must be valid for the period of time you are applying to study for.

(b) A completed and signed **Application for Student Visa** form, with a passport-size photograph. You will be required to pay a non-refundable student visa application fee of NZ$188.00.

(c) A written offer of a place, which notifies you that you have been accepted by an educational institution in New Zealand to undertake a course of study.

(d) Either a receipt for payment of course fees (you are not required to produce the receipt before your application has been approved in principle), or evidence that you are exempt from course fees, *eg* by a New Zealand Government Scholarship. To find out more about this please contact your nearest New Zealand Embassy office.

(e) A guarantee of accommodation – a written assurance from an educational institution or other person, that suitable residential accommodation is available to you in New Zealand.

(f) Evidence that funds are available for your maintenance

throughout your stay. The following is acceptable –

- A completed **Sponsoring a Student** form, in which your sponsor gives a financial undertaking that he or she can transfer to New Zealand approximately NZ$7,000 per year.

- A letter from your educational institution confirming that your living costs have already been paid.

- A bank document showing the funds of the amount required will be available to you in New Zealand *eg* approximately NZ$1,000 for each month of your stay for short-term study, or approximately NZ$7,000 per year for long-term study.

- An award of a full New Zealand scholarship.

(g) Evidence of arrangements for onward travel from New Zealand. If you are undertaking a long-term course, a completed **Sponsoring a Student** form will usually satisfy this requirement. If you intend taking a short-term course, you will need to provide a return ticket to show that you have the funds to do so.

If you intend studying in New Zealand for more than two years you will need to show New Zealand Immigration Service medical and chest X-ray certificates, plus character clearances, which must be:

- two original character references if under 17 years of age or

- a local police clearance if you are 17 years of age and over. You will be advised of the procedure for obtaining these by the New Zealand Government office of your country.

All of the above are essential before a student visa is issued. When the New Zealand Government office overseas is satisfied that your application is complete and in order you will be issued a student visa.

If your course of study is less than three months, a student visa is not required.

If you are in New Zealand, or entering New Zealand on a visitor's visa, or under a visa-waiver agreement, or as the dependant of a visitor for a short time, you may be admitted to a primary or secondary school without charge for a period of up to 28 consecutive days, at the discretion of the principal and beyond 28 days with the approval of the Secretary of Education.

Permits

When you arrive in New Zealand your passport will be endorsed with a permit which will allow you to be here for study or training whilst it is current. If you need an extension of your permit, you must apply before the original permit expires. Failure to do so will mean that you are here unlawfully, and may be removed. If you leave New Zealand before your permit expires, it will automatically cancel.

Further information for students

New Zealand Immigration Service will issue a visa or permit to a school student for one year, on the basis of one term's fees. However, if an instalment of fees is for less than one term, a visa or permit will be issued for only the period covered by the instalment. A permit renewal fee is payable.

If you wish to transfer to another course or institution, you must obtain a variation to your student permit, specifying the course and institution and, if appropriate, the extended validity of the permit.

Health benefits for students

As a full-fee foreign student you are eligible for health benefits if your course of study is of two or more years' duration. It is strongly recommended that all foreign students obtain medical insurance cover, especially students on shorter course of up to two years' duration. Information on medical insurance will be available from New Zealand Government offices overseas.

Full-fee students from the United Kingdom and Australia are eligible for health benefits during courses of study lasting less than two years if they meet the requirements of the reciprocal health agreements New Zealand has with these countries.

Income support

You will not be eligible for income support assistance. A condition of your student visa is that you will be able to meet the full costs of education, accommodation and other living costs.

Accident compensation

You will be eligible for accident compensation on the same basis as resident New Zealand citizens. This will include earnings-related compensation if you are working.

KEY FEATURES

1. Last date by which holder must arrive in New Zealand
2. Issued for multiple/single journeys
3. Usually children travelling on the same passport may be included here
4. Limiting factors such as occupation or place of study may be inserted here

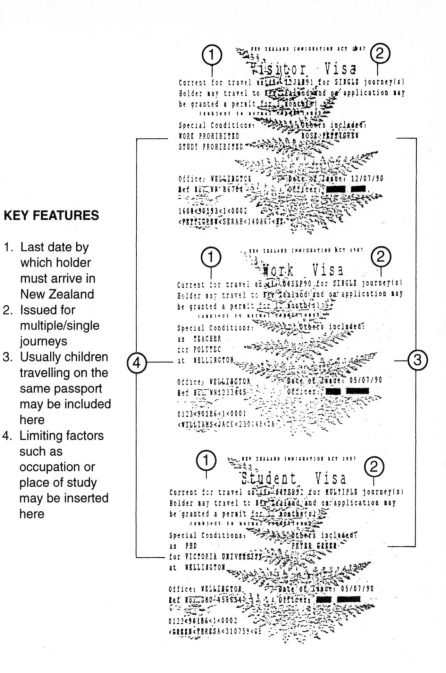

Fig. 5. Examples of New Zealand visas.

KEY FEATURES

1. Date on which permit comes into force
2. Date permit expires
3. Usually children travelling on the same passport may be included here
4. Limiting factors such as occupation or place of study may be inserted here

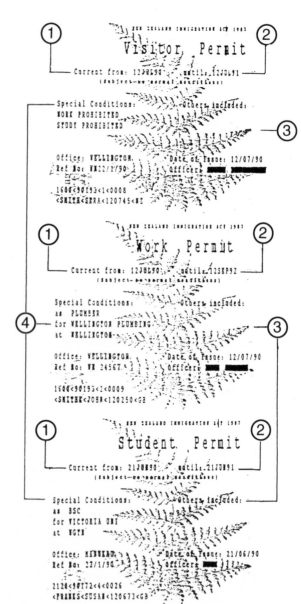

Fig. 6. Examples of New Zealand permits.

Student allowances
Foreign students will not be entitled to student loans or to allowances under the Student Allowances Regulations 1991. Australian citizens or those who have been granted the right to reside permanently in Australia will be entitled to student loans. They may also apply for student allowances provided they make a statutory declaration of their intention to reside permanently in New Zealand.

Restrictions on student employment
Holiday employment
You need to apply for special permission from the nearest office of the New Zealand Immigration Service before you commence holiday employment. You may work only during the long summer holidays and only if you are taking a full-time course of more than 12 months' duration.

Course related employment
The New Zealand Immigration Service will grant approval for you to work during the year if it is work experience related to course requirements. They may also give you permission to remain in New Zealand and work for up to two years in employment related to your course if it has not been possible to gain work experience during your studies and if this work experience is a condition of being awarded a certificate.

Application for spouses of students to work
If your spouse wishes to work while you are in New Zealand, an application must be made through an office of the New Zealand Immigration Service. (See the addresses at the back of this book.)

Decisions on applications will depend on whether there are any unemployed New Zealand residents who can do the job which has been offered. For this reason, no definite assurance can be given whether an application would be successful.

Postgraduate study
If you have already completed an undergraduate course at a New Zealand university, you can apply for a further permit to do postgraduate study.

OBTAINING A WORK PERMIT

Anyone who arranges a job before arriving in New Zealand, or who intends to come to New Zealand to work, must apply in their own country for a work visa. Do not make arrangements to travel here until you have written approval of your application.

How to apply

If you have a current work, visitor's or student permit and you now want a work permit to stay longer, you must apply before your current permit expires. Your work permit application will be considered according to the local job market. A permit will normally be issued only if a suitable New Zealand citizen or resident is not available locally for the job.

You will need to supply:

- a completed **Application for Work Permit**

- your passport or certificate of identity, which must be valid for one month beyond the proposed date of leaving New Zealand, or three months if your passport has to be sent outside New Zealand for renewal

- a recent passport-size photo

- the application fee.

The person or firm offering you the job must provide you with the following information in writing to give to the New Zealand Immigration Service:

- the name, address, telephone and/or fax number of company or employer

- a job description including –
Job title
Type of work or duties
Pay and conditions
Qualifications or training or experience required
Duration of the job
Details of attempts to recruit New Zealanders and reasons why none was suitable.

You must supply evidence that you are suitably qualified by training and experience to do the job, and if the salary or pay from your prospective employer is not considered enough to cover your maintenance and/or outward travel, you may also be asked to produce evidence of money or means of support and an outward ticket or other evidence of the travel arrangements you have made to leave at the end of your stay. It is very important that you make a careful note of the expiry date of your permit, because if you stay in New Zealand after that date you will be here unlawfully and will be liable for removal.

Other conditions of a work permit
You may not study without obtaining:

- a student permit, or

- a change to the conditions of your work permit to let you study for a short time,

unless the course is one single course of not more than three months' duration.

United Kingdom Working Holiday Scheme
British residents aged between 18 and 30, and unaccompanied by children, are allowed to have one-year working holidays in New Zealand, under the **Temporary Work Permit Scheme**.

New Zealand allows 500 people per year, on a first come first served basis. All applicants have to satisfy the New Zealand Immigration officers in London that their primary intention is to holiday in New Zealand. They are then only allowed to perform 'incidental or temporary work' whilst in New Zealand.

PERMANENT MIGRANTS

There are four main categories permanent migrants will be considered under:

- General Skills Category
- Business Investment Category
- Family Category
- Humanitarian Category.

General migrant category

The general category replaces the former occupational system with a 'points system' which ranks applicants on their qualifications, work experience, age and settlement factors. A minimum level of the English language is also a requirement.

The emphasis of this category is on assessing the overall standard of the applicant, with migrants being allocated points for experience and skills and then assessed accordingly. Those gaining the highest number of points will be eligible for residence, provided they satisfy the normal immigration criteria.

The main areas tested will be –

- *Employability*
  This is the major element and will relate to qualifications and work experience. You will need to supply *original* or *certified* true copies of your qualifications, and evidence that you were employed in your stated occupation for the given length of time.

- *Qualifications*
  The following rules apply:
  – You can only obtain points for one qualification.
  – Partially completed qualifications will not be accepted.
  – Your qualifications must be of a comparable standard to a New Zealand qualification.

Note: in New Zealand there are certain occupations for which you must have membership of and/or registration with a professional or industrial organisation. Some examples of such occupations are:

Dental technicians	Optometrists	Radio/TV servicing personnel
Electricians	Pharmacists	Town planners
Lawyers	Plumbers and	Veterinarians
Medical personnel	gas fitters	

If you wish to apply for residence in New Zealand you do not have to be registered. If you are registered, however, this will assist the New Zealand Immigration Service in making a correct assessment of your qualification (see Chapter 3).

Work experience
You can score points for work experience that is:

- sound, continuous and relevant to your qualification (which you obtained after the completion of your schooling) for which you by obtain points.

Your work experience must have been obtained after you completed your qualification, or be:

- sound, continuous and in an approved occupation.

An approved occupation is one which is considered skilled in New Zealand and appears on the New Zealand Immigration Service's Register of Approved Occupations. To score points in this area you must have had at least five years' experience in your approved occupation. You may wish to contact your local New Zealand Immigration Service office for advice on whether you are working in an approved occupation.

Note: if you have a post-schooling qualification and work experience which is not directly related to that qualification, you cannot claim points for both the work experience and the qualification, even if the work experience is in an approved occupation. You can, however, claim points for both twelve years' schooling and work experience in an approved occupation.

Age
You will be allocated points for the age that you are at the time you lodge your application. If you are over the maximum age limit of 55 years, you are not eligible to be approved under the General Category.

Settlement factors
If you claim points for settlement funds, your investment funds must be additional to your settlement funds.

Settlement funds
To score points, your settlement funds (*ie* the value of your house, cash, shares, stocks find any other assets, minus all your debts) *must* be worth at least NZ$100,000.

Investment funds
To score points you must have between NZ$100,000 and NZ$300,000 and must be willing and able to have it transferred to, and invested in, New Zealand for at least two years. This

investment must, in normal circumstances, provide a commercial return on the funds invested. Applicants will not be permitted to invest the funds in the purchase of possessions that could be for personal use, such as a house or car.

Note: you should note that settlement funds of $100,000 will attract two points, while the same amount of investment funds attract one point.

Sponsorship
To score points for a sponsor, you must have a family sponsor who is your adult brother or sister, or parent, or adult child, who is a New Zealand resident, who has been lawfully permanently living in New Zealand for at least three years immediately prior to the application, and is prepared to accept family sponsorship obligations.

Your community sponsor must be prepared to accept community sponsorship obligations, and be approved by the New Zealand Immigration Service.

Offer of skilled employment
To score points for an offer of skilled employment, you must have a firm and genuine job offer which will be kept open for six months. (For further details contact your nearest Immigration Office.)

Business and investment migrant category
The Government recognises that business migrants can significantly add to the wealth of New Zealand, and as a result, consideration will be given to applicants with substantial capital and business skills who can create jobs and enhance development.

Applicants in this category will be required to bring into New Zealand a minimum of NZ$750,000.

Though in general business migrants will be allowed to place their money in investments of their choice, a residence visa will *not* be granted until funds have been lodged in a New Zealand investment, and if those funds are not kept there for at least two years, the residence permit may be revoked.

Applicants must be able to show that the business investment funds are the direct result of their own business or professional record over a period of at least three years, and that their business or professional record extends over a minimum period of ten years. This category will be open to business people of all ages, and will require a minimum level of English language ability on the part of the principal applicant or their spouse or an adult child over 17.

Self assessment
Having got this far you must be anxious to see if you will qualify. This you can do by using the Self Assessment Form on page 48.

General skills category
The emphasis of the general skills category is on assessing the overall human capital of the applicant, with migrants being allocated points for attributes and then periodically ranked (if you score 24 points or less, your application will be declined). Those scoring the higher number of points may be eligible for residence, *provided they satisfy the normal immigration criteria.* Contact the New Zealand Immigration Service for the current pass mark.

After having scored a pass mark, you will now need to get the necessary **Application For Residence in New Zealand** forms from a New Zealand Immigration Office (see the addresses at the back of book).

Business investor category
The aim of the business investor category is to ensure that high quality migrants with excellent, proven business skills and experience gain entry to New Zealand. Generally, they are also expected to invest business funds in New Zealand. You will be granted residence under the business investor category if you score enough points to meet the pass mark and you meet the compulsory requirements. Contact the New Zealand Immigration Service for the current pass mark.

Family migrant category
This category covers three situations – marriage to a New Zealand citizen or resident; de facto/homosexual relationship with a citizen or resident; parents, dependent children and single adult brothers and sisters and children. A legally married spouse of a New Zealand resident or citizen may qualify for residence. De facto or homosexual partners of New Zealand citizens or residents may be considered for residence. Once again, approval is not automatic, and an interview with both partners may be held. The couple will need to show they are living together in a stable, lasting relationship. The relationship must be of at least two years' duration in the case of a de facto couple, and four years if the relationship is homosexual.

Self assessment

POINTS FACTOR	POINTS		YOUR SCORE	
	You	Spouse	You	Spouse

EMPLOYABILITY FACTORS
Points may be scored for both Qualifications and
Work Experience
 	
1. Qualifications:
   Any equivalent to a base degree,
   trade or 3 yr diploma/certificate
   Any advanced trade or professional qualification
   Any equivalent of a Masters or better
	
	10
	11
	12
		
		1
		–
		2		

2. Work Experience:
   (Must be relevant to Post Secondary
   Qualifications or in an Approved Occupation)
 	
   2 complete years
   4 complete years
   6 complete years
   8 complete years
  10 complete years
  12 complete years
  14 complete years
  16 complete years
  18 complete years
  20 complete years
 	
Maximum points for Employability factor: 25
	
	1
	2
	3
	4
	5
	6
	7
	8
	9
	10			

3. Age:
 	
   18-24 years
   25-29 years
   30-34 years
   35-39 years
   40-44 years
   45-49 years
   Maximum age limit: 55 years
 	
Maximum points for Age factor: 10
	
	8
	10
	8
	6
	4
	2			

4. Settlement Factors:
   NZ$100,000 settlement funds (max 2 points)
   Family sponsor
   1 point for each additional NZ$100,000
   investments funds, up to a max of $300,000
   Offer of Skilled employment (full time)
	
	1
	3
	
	3
	5			

MAXIMUM POINTS: 40 **TOTAL:**				

Fig. 7. General category – points system.

If you are a parent, you are eligible to be reunited with your adult children in New Zealand (provided all your adult children are living permanently outside your home country, or you have an equal or greater number of adult children lawfully permanently resident in New Zealand than anywhere else).

Limited provisions exist for parents with dependent children. Single adult brothers, sisters and children of New Zealand citizens or residents (including persons who are divorced or widowed) are eligible for residence provided they have no children and have no immediate family in their home country.

If you are applying under family reunification you will need a sponsor or support from the New Zealand based relative.

Unmarried dependent children under 17 are eligible for residence if they:

- are joining their parent(s) in New Zealand
- have no children of their own
- were declared in their parents' application for residence, and provided their parents are lawfully and permanently living in New Zealand.

APPEALS

There are two appeal authorities which can review declined applications.

The **Residence Appeal Authority** will provide unsuccessful residence applicants with an opportunity to have the decision independently reviewed. The Authority may approve cases where it is satisfied they fall within policy.

The **Removal Review Authority** will have the power to quash a removal order where there are exceptional humanitarian grounds for allowing the person to remain in New Zealand, or where a person has been determined not to be an overstayer.

There is provision for appeals on questions of law to be taken to the High Court.

Provision is also made in the Immigration Act for the reconsideration of any refusal by an immigration officer to grant a temporary permit.

IMMIGRATION FEES

- The fees apply from 1 July 1994.
- Your application will not be considered unless the correct fee is paid.

Family applications

Your spouse and unmarried dependent children under 20 years of age do not need to make a separate application and pay a separate fee if they are included in your application for –

- a visitor's visa or a visitor's permit
- a returning resident's visa
- a transit visa
- a residence visa or residence permit.

Children of 17 years or older who are not dependent, and all children of 20 years or over, must make their own application for any type of visa or permit, and must pay a separate fee.

There is no charge for your first permit, which is granted on arrival in New Zealand.

The fee you must pay when lodging an application covers the cost of processing. Payment of the fee does not mean the application will be approved.

Approximate fees

	NZ$
Residence Visa	
(a) Business immigration category	2,255.00
(b) Other categories	635.00
Residence Permit	
(a) Business immigration category	2,255.00
(b) Other categories	618.00

Business immigration category application fees do not include Goods and Services Tax (GST) as they are assessed outside New Zealand. GST (12.5%) is payable when the service is provided in New Zealand.

Returning resident's visa	50.00
Visitor's visa[1]	60.00

Visitor's permit[2]	60.00
Work visa[1]	130.00
Work permit[2]	130.00
Student visa[1]	190.00
Student permit[2]	70.00
Application for reconsideration of decision to decline another temporary permit	140.00
Application for a special direction to vary the conditions of a temporary permit	140.00
Making of special direction to grant a permit or apply any exemption to a person to whom section 7(1) of the Act applies	140.00

Lodging of appeal
(a) To Residence Appeal Authority under
     section 18c of the Act   510.00

(b) To Removal Review Authority under
     section 63A of the Act   510.00

(c) To Removal Review Authority under
     section 63B of the Act   510.00

(d) To Minister of Immigration under
     section 63 of the Act (being an appeal lodged
     pursuant to section 34 of the Immigration
     Amendment Act 1991).   510.00

Notes
[1] You apply for a visa if you are
     (a) applying to come to New Zealand, or
     (b) already in New Zealand and want to leave and then return.
[2] You apply for a permit if you are already in New Zealand and
     want to extend your stay.

OBTAINING A POLICE CERTIFICATE

All applicants applying for residence in New Zealand must provide a
Police Certificate at the same time as a residence application is
lodged. This Certificate must be less than two months old at the time

the application is lodged.

You must apply for this from your country of residence, but contact the nearest New Zealand Immigration office. If you have lived for periods of 12 months or more in other countries during the last ten years, you must obtain certificates from these countries also. The certificates must be in English, or on an official letterhead as a certified translation, with a stamp or signature of the translator.

HUMANITARIAN CATEGORY

This covers people whose circumstances are exceptionally difficult. The applicant must have at least one close relative who is a New Zealand citizen or resident, and who supports the application. Applicants will be assessed under the following criteria:

- their circumstances must be such that they, or a New Zealand party, is suffering serious physical or emotional harm, and

- their application is supported by a close family member who is a New Zealand citizen or resident, and

- they produce evidence to show why their situation can only be resolved by their being granted residence in New Zealand, and

- it would not be contrary to the public interest to allow the applicants to reside in New Zealand.

A close family member is defined for the purposes of the Humanitarian Category as a parent, sibling or child, aunt, uncle, nephew, niece, grandparent or a person who has lived with, and been part of, the applicant's family for many years.

QUESTIONS AND ANSWERS ON IMMIGRATION

How long does it take to process residence applicants?

It can take up to six months. However, if you ensure that your application is complete and all the necessary material is enclosed with your application, *ie* original documents or certified copies, then you stand a much better chance of getting an early reply.

If I pass the 'points system' does this automatically guarantee a job?

No, access is by no means a guarantee of a job.

How can I find out about work prospects?

By obtaining New Zealand newspapers or by contacting your nearest Immigration Office. You could also contact an Employment Bureau in New Zealand (see end of book for addresses). If funds allow, you could always come here first on a visitor's visa to check the situation out for yourself before applying for New Zealand residency and selling up in your homeland.

Is it possible that a visitor wouldn't be allowed a permit upon arrival in New Zealand?

Yes, but only if something unusual had happened in between your getting your visa and your arrival in New Zealand.

INWARDS AND OUTWARDS MIGRATION

The flow of people isn't just inwards into New Zealand. Several New Zealanders have had to abandon, temporarily or otherwise, their country of birth to earn a living overseas.

Rachael Hunter, who is a photographers' model, made her name as a very highly paid model in America. She met Rod Stewart, famous English pop singer, they got married, and now she lives permanently in England. She would have had to live 'outside' New Zealand even if she hadn't met Rocker Rod.

Sam Neill, the sexy superstar, started off small time acting in New Zealand, but he didn't achieve world fame and fortune until he went overseas. Now he just comes home for a visit to 'wind down'.

Kiri Te Kanawa, the world acclaimed opera singer, went overseas for furtherance of her career, and now lives outside London. She, too, is just an occasional visitor to these shores.

Bob Charles, well-known golf champion, now travels overseas to play the golf circuits as a veteran golfer. He earns his income overseas, and very rarely competes in New Zealand. He does come back to his New Zealand home occasionally.

NEW ZEALAND
IMMIGRATION SERVICE

IMMIGRATION ACT 1987

Application for Visitor's Visa

If you want to:
■ **Work in New Zealand** - use form *Application for Work Visa*
■ **Study or undertake training** - use form *Application for Student Visa*
■ **Settle in New Zealand** - use form *Application for Residence in New Zealand*

Please read these notes:

❑ Read the leaflet *Visiting New Zealand* before completing this form.

❑ This form must be completed in English.

❑ There is no charge for this form.

❑ Your spouse and unmarried dependent children under 20 years of age do not need to make a separate application and pay a separate fee if they are included in your application for a visitor's visa.

❑ Children 17 or older who are not dependent, and all children 20 years of age and over, must make their own application for a visitor's visa and pay a separate fee.

❑ You must enclose the correct application fee (see the leaflet *New Zealand Immigration Fees*) unless:
■ you are from a country which has a **visa waiver** agreement with New Zealand, and you do not need a visa because you intend to visit only for the time stated in the agreement, or
■ you are from a country which has a **visa fee waiver** agreement with New Zealand. (Countries which have visa waiver **or** visa fee waiver agreements with New Zealand are listed in our leaflet *Visiting New Zealand*)

❑ If you make any false statements you commit an offence and your application may be declined, or (if you have travelled to New Zealand) your permit may be revoked.

Please answer all the questions

1 **Your surname or family name?** As shown in your Passport or Certificate of Identity

2 **Your first or given names?** As shown in your Passport or Certificate of Identity

3 **Any other name(s) you are known by?**

4 **Your name in ethnic script?**

5 **Your sex?**
Please answer MALE or FEMALE

6 **Your place of birth?**

7 **Your country of birth?**

8 **Your marital status?**
Show below which status applies to you
■ never married ■ now married ■ engaged
■ widowed ■ separated ■ divorced ■ de facto

9 **Your date of birth?**
day   month   year

From your Passport or Certificate of Identity give the answer to questions 10 to 12 below

10 **Your Passport/Certificate of Identity number?**

11 **What date does your Passport/Certificate of Identity expire?**
day   month   year

12 **Your citizenship?**

13 **Details of spouse and any children included in this application.**
Name as shown in spouse or child's Passport or Travel Document | Passport No | Citizenship | Date of birth day month year | Relationship to applicant (for example son, daughter)

Fig. 8. Application for a visitor's visa.

14 If any other family members travelling with you are applying separately for visas, please give the following details:

Name as shown in their Passport or Travel Document — Type of visa applied for — Citizenship — Relationship to applicant (for example: wife, husband)

15 Have you or any family member been to New Zealand before?   *Please answer YES or NO*

If YES, say when, for how long and the type of permit you held.

Name as shown in their Passport or Travel Document — Permit type held — Date of arrival in New Zealand day month year — Date of departure from New Zealand day month year

16 When are you leaving to go to New Zealand?

17 When do you expect to arrive in New Zealand?

18 How long do you intend to stay in New Zealand?
Months   Weeks   Days

19 What is the main reason for your visit to New Zealand?

20 Do you have a ticket for leaving New Zealand?

Please answer YES or NO

If NO, give details of the arrangements you have made to leave New Zealand.

21 How do you intend to support yourself and any dependents for the length of your stay in New Zealand?
(See leaflet *Visiting New Zealand* for a guide to how much money you should have or sponsorship arrangements)

22 What is your usual occupation?

23 If employed, who do you work for?
Give name and address of employer

24 Your usual residential address?

25 Can you be telephoned during the day?

Please answer YES or NO

If YES give your day-time telephone number (include area code)

26 Your address where all mail to do with this application should be sent?

27 How do you want your papers returned to you?
Please answer BY COLLECTION or BY MAIL

Fig. 8. Continued.

55

28 Do you have relatives, friends, business or other personal contacts in New Zealand?

Please answer YES or NO   *If YES give details below:*

Name   Address   Relationship to applicant

29 Do you, or any other person included in this application, intend seeking medical treatment while visiting New Zealand?

Please answer YES or NO

*If Yes please read the information leaflet **Visiting New Zealand** and complete and attach the form **Details of Intended Medical Treatment** to this application.*

30 When you leave New Zealand, have you the right of re-entry to your usual country of residence?

Please answer YES or NO

31 Have you ever been convicted of any offence(s) against the law in any country?

Please answer YES or NO

If **YES** give details of nature of offence(s), year convicted and penalty imposed.

32 Have you ever been deported, excluded from or ordered to leave any country, including New Zealand ?

Please answer YES or NO

*If **YES** say where, when and why*

33 Have you ever been refused a visa or permit for any country, including New Zealand?

Please answer YES or NO

*If **YES** say where, when and why*

Declaration

I understand the notes and questions in this form **and**
the information given is true and complete.

Signature of applicant

date

Signature of parent or guardian
(if applicant aged under 17 years)

date

To be completed by any person who has assisted applicant to complete this form.

Full name of interpreter / agent

Address of interpreter / agent

I certify that I have completed this and any attached forms at the request of the applicant **and**
the applicant understood the content of the form(s) and the answers given and approved them before signing the declaration.

Signature of interpreter / agent

date

.Fig. 8. Continued.

NEW ZEALAND
IMMIGRATION SErViCE

Application for Student Visa

Please read these notes:

- Read the leaflet *Getting a Student Visa* before completing this form.

- This form must be completed in English.

- This form is given free of charge.

- You will need to enclose the application fee, which is non-refundable, when you lodge this form. See the leaflet *New Zealand Immigration Fees.*

- If you make any false statements in your application, you commit an offence and your application may be declined or your permit to be in New Zealand may be revoked.

Please answer all the questions.

1   **Your full name?** As shown in your Passport or Certificate of Identity

Please underline your Family Name or Surname

2   **Any other name you are known by?**

3   **Your usual residential address?**

4   **Details of parents or guardian?**

Name of Father   Address

Name of Mother   Address

Name of Guardian (if applicable)   Address

5   **Do you have a spouse?** A spouse could be a wife, husband or de facto partner.

Please answer **YES** or **NO** _____   If **YES** give details below

Name of spouse   Spouse's date of birth   Travelling with you ?

                                                        day   month   year

6   **Do you have children?**

Please answer **YES** or **NO** _____   If **YES** give details below

                                                                Date of birth
Name of child   Male or female   day   month   year   Travelling with you?

7   **Do you have relatives, friends or other personal contacts in New Zealand?**

Please answer **YES** or **NO** _____   If **YES** give details below

Name   Address   Relationship to applicant

Fig. 9. Application for a student visa.

8 Your sex?
   Please answer MALE or FEMALE

9 Your date of birth?

   day   month   year

10 Your country of birth?

From your Passport or Certificate of Identity
give the answers to questions 11 to 13 below

---

11 Your Passport/Certificate of Identity number?

12 What date does your Passport/ Certificate
   of Identity expire?

   day   month   year

13 Your citizenship?

14 What course or courses do you want to take?

15 What qualification do you want to get?

16 What is the starting date of your course in
   New Zealand?

   day   month   year

17 What arrangements have been made for your
   accommodation in New Zealand?

18 What provision has been made for your fare to
   leave New Zealand ?

19 Have you any physical or mental disability or
   special care needs?

   Please answer YES or NO

   *If YES give a brief description of your disability and
   any medical treatment being given.*

20 When you leave New Zealand, have you the right of
   re-entry to your usual country of residence?

   Please answer YES or NO

21 Have you ever been convicted of any offence
   against the law in any country?

   Please answer YES or NO

   *If YES give details of nature of offence, year
   convicted and penalty imposed.*

22 Have you ever been deported, excluded from or
   ordered to leave any country?

   Please answer YES or NO

   If YES say where, when and why

23 Can you be telephoned during the day ?

   Please answer YES or NO

   *If YES give your day-time
   telephone number
   (include Area Code)*

24 Your address where all mail to do with
   this application should be sent?

Fig. 9. Continued.

25 How do you want your documents returned to you?

Please answer
BY COLLECTION or
BY MAIL

Declaration

I understand the notes and questions in this form
and
the information given is true and complete.

Signature of applicant

date

Signature of parent or guardian
(if applicant aged under 17 years).

date

What to do next ?

⊐ Attach to this application a recent passport
photograph of yourself with your name on the back.

⊐ Attach your notice of acceptance into an approved
course of study or training if you have it . The notice
should show:

   ⊐ name and address of institution
   ⊐ course of study offered
   ⊐ minimum length of course

⊐ Attach two character references *plus* local
police clearance if requested.

⊐ Attach financial undertaking.

Have you

Enclosed the application fee?

Enclosed your Passport or Certificate of
Identity?

Attached your photograph to this application?

Signed the Declaration?

**To be completed by any person who has
assisted applicant to complete this form.**

Full name of interpreter / agent

Address of interpreter / agent

I certify that I have completed this and any attached
forms at the request of the applicant
and
the applicant understood the content of the form(s)
and the answers given and approved them before
signing the declaration.

Signature of interpreter / agent

date

```
┌ ─ ─ ─ ─ ┐
│         │
│ Attach your │
│ Passport  │
│ Photograph │
│ here      │
└ ─ ─ ─ ─ ┘
```

Issued by the Immigration Division of the Department of Labour,
Wellington, New Zealand.

NZIS-267

Fig. 9. Continued.

59

NEW ZEALAND IMMIGRATION SERVICE
Application for Work Visa

IMMIGRATION ACT 1987

If you want to:

■ Visit only while in New Zealand - use form *Application for Visitor's Visa*
■ Study or undertake training - use form *Application for Student Visa*
■ Settle in New Zealand - use form *Application for Residence*

Please read these notes:

⬜ Read the leaflet *Getting a Work Visa* before completing this form.

⬜ If you have a letter from your proposed employer offering employment, send it in with your application.

⬜ This form must be completed in English.

⬜ You will need to enclose the application fee, which is non-refundable, when you lodge this form. See leaflet *New Zealand Immigration Fees*.

⬜ If you make any false statements you commit an offence and your application may be declined or your permit to be in New Zealand may be revoked.

⬜ This form is given free of charge.

Please answer all the questions

---

1 **Your full name ?** As shown in your Passport or Certificate of Identity

Please underline your Family name or Surname

2 **Any other name you are known by?**

3 **Your usual residential address?**

4 **Details of family members travelling with you.**
Name as shown in their Passport or Certificate of Identity

Relationship to applicant (for example: wife, husband)

Type of Visa applied for (if any)

5 **What type of work do you want to do in New Zealand?**

6 **Do you have a written offer of employment in New Zealand?**

Please answer YES or NO

If YES give name and address of proposed employer or agent in New Zealand

Fig. 10. Application for a work visa.

60

7 Your sex ?
Please answer MALE or FEMALE

8 Your date of birth ?

                        day   month   year

9 Your country of birth ?

10 Your marital status?
    Show below which status applies to you
      ■ never married   ■ now married
      ■ widowed   ■ separated   ■ divorced

From your Passport or Certificate of Identity give the answer to questions 11 to 13 below

11 Your Passport/Certificate of Identity number?

12 What date does your Passport/Certificate of Identity expire?

                        day   month   year

13 Your citizenship?

14 When are you leaving to go to New Zealand?

15 When do you expect to arrive in New Zealand?

16 How long do you intend to stay in New Zealand?
        years   months

17 Have you been to New Zealand within the last 2 years?
    Please answer YES or NO

18 When you leave New Zealand, have you the right of re-entry to your usual country of residence?
    Please answer YES or NO

19 What arrangements have been made for your return or outward ticket?

20 Have you any physical or mental disability or special care needs?
    Please answer YES or NO

    If YES give a brief description of your disability and any medical treatment being given.

21 Have you ever been convicted of any offence against the law in any country?
    Please answer YES or NO

    If YES give details of nature of offence, year convicted and penalty imposed.

22 Have you ever been deported, excluded from or ordered to leave any country?
    Please answer YES or NO

    If YES say where, when and why

Fig. 10. Continued.

23 Can you be telephoned during the day?

Please answer YES or NO

If YES give your day-time
telephone number
(Include area code)

24 Your address where all mail to do with this
application should be sent?

25 How do you want your papers returned to you?
Please answer
BY COLLECTION or
BY MAIL

Declaration

I understand the notes and questions in this form
and
the information given is true and complete

Signature of applicant

date

What to do next?

Please attach to this application a recent passport
photograph of yourself with your name on the back.

Have you

Enclosed the application fee?

Attached a written offer of employment?

Enclosed your Passport or Certificate of Identity?

Attached your photograph to this application?

Signed the Declaration?

To be completed by any person who has
assisted applicant to complete this form.

Full name of interpreter / agent

Address of interpreter / agent

I certify that I have completed this and any attached
forms at the request of the applicant
and
the applicant understood the content of the form(s)
and the answers given and approved them before
signing the declaration.

Signature of interpreter / agent

date

```
┌ ─ ─ ─ ─ ─ ┐
│ Attach your │
│ Passport    │
│ Photograph  │
│ here        │
│             │
└ ─ ─ ─ ─ ─ ┘
```

Issued by the Immigration Division of the Department of Labour
Wellington, New Zealand

NZIS 2?

Fig. 10. Continued.

3

Earning a Dollar

JOB HUNTING

Unlike Australia, New Zealand does not maintain an occupations list, *ie* a list of preferred professionals and likely job vacancies.

The New Zealand Immigration Department does not feel it would be helpful to issue such a list, as it would be continually out of date. The preferred system is for a person to qualify with the points system. If for instance they issued a list saying that the country was in need of electronic engineers, by the time the list was circulated, it would probably be out of date and New Zealand would then be overrun with electronic engineers insisting that they were needed!

More graduates but fewer jobs

More students graduate each year, but job prospects have not kept pace. Statistics show that in 1998, people with jobs were more likely to have qualifications than those without jobs. Unemployment rates were higher for those without qualifications – 11.5% was the unemployment rate for those without qualifications, compared with 6.3% for those with qualifications.

Those working as legislators, administrators, managers, technicians and associate professionals had the highest proportion of people with qualifications – all over 80%. Those without qualifications were more likely to work in elementary occupations as plant and machine operators and assemblers.

LABOUR RELATIONS

On 15 May 1991 the new Government repealed the Labour Relations Act 1987 and enacted the **Employment Contracts Act**.

This Act provided a fundamentally different framework for the conduct of industrial relations. Rather than being based on a conflict model of industrial relations, it is based on two quite different assumptions:

- Employers and their employees have a mutual interest in maintaining the wealth and profitability of their enterprises.

- Employers and their employees are in the best position to make decisions on what arrangements should govern their employment relationship.

To achieve these ends, the Act removes union monopolies over coverage and bargaining; it gives employees the right to decide whether or not they wish to belong to an employee organisation such as a union and the right to choose who, if anybody, they want to represent them. It aims to encourage bargaining outcomes that are relevant to the work place and enables employers and employees to negotiate either individual or collective employment contracts directly.

Employees are now required to sign an **employment contract**. Bargaining can be done by the person involved, or they may elect to have someone bargain for them. A bargaining agent must not have been convicted of an offence punishable by five years or more in prison, within the last ten years.

No smoking
It is not unusual to see groups of people standing outside office blocks smoking. This is because many offices now have a ban on smoking, so the people who smoke have to go outside when they want a quick 'drag'. When applying for a job you will quite possibly be asked if you smoke, and you will probably find that a condition of the job is that you do not smoke.

FINDING A JOB

There are three ways in which to track down the 'right' job:

- the newspapers
- New Zealand Employment Bureau
- private employment bureaux.

The newspapers
Write to a New Zealand newspaper office, enquiring as to the cost of sending you the latest editions, or view the latest news online.

The New Zealand Herald, Box 32, Auckland. Website: *www.nzherald.co.nz*
The Dominion, Box 1297, Wellington
The Otago Times, Box 517 Dunedin
The Christchurch Star, Box 1467, Christchurch.

It would be a good idea to mention that you are interested in 'situations vacant' and would therefore like the issue with the largest selection – Saturday for some papers and Wednesday/Thursday for others.

New Zealand Employment Service
These offices are run by the Labour Department, and their main purpose is to help people find work. Unlike the private employment bureaux, the New Zealand Employment Bureau does not make a charge. The offices are as follows:

New Zealand Employment Service:

PO Box 23 358, Auckland. Tel: 64-9-278 0905.
PO Box 5065, Whangarei. Tel: 64-09-438 8875.
PO Box 9446, Wellington. Tel: 64-4-81 5277.
PO Box 4441,Christchurch. Tel: 64-3-377 0530.
PO Box 859, Dunedin. Tel: 64-3-477 5395.
PO Box 545, Napier. Tel: 64-6-835 8569.

Private employment bureaux
There are many employment bureaux, and some of them specialise in different areas, so here are a few of the larger and better known:

Hospitality industry
Kelly Services (NZ) Ltd. Box 10151, Wellington. Tel: 64-4-499 2825. Fax: 64-4-499 2821.
Hotel & Leisure Resources Ltd. Box 5881, Wellesley St, Auckland. Tel: 64-9-358 4980.

Two major hotel chains you could try:

Quality Hotels, Box 5640, Wellesley St, Auckland. Tel: 64-9-309 4411. Fax: 64-9-377 0764.

Southern Pacific Hotel Corporation, Box 3921, Auckland. Tel: 64-9-373 2269.

Fig. 11. Some typical New Zealand job advertisements.

OCCUPATIONAL HEALTH NURSE

Registered Nurse required OCC health experience an advantage to manage contracts in the Auckland area, 10-15 hours pw.

NATION WIDE PROMOTION Co

seeks too sales people, 13 week promotion. Travel and promotion opportunities abound

RECEPTIONIST

Part-time and full-time receptionists required for Boutique Hotel and Conference Centre. Position is on a rotating roster which involves am and pm shifts as well as some weekends. Candidates must have:

RECEPTIONIST/TYPIST

Newmarket professional office, front desk position, excellent telephone manner required, copy word processing reports and letters in Word 97, data entry using accounts software, mail, banking, other duties, cheerful working environment, good team, please reply in writing to:

LANDSCAPER

Experienced landscape gardener wanted, must be able to run job and gang, excellent rate for right person. Only genuine applicants need apply.

KITCHEN HAND

Required for Parnell Restaurant, Mon to Sat nights, 6 mths exper, immed start.

MACHINIST

Experienced machinists required for busy Swimwear Company. Must be skilled on coverstitch and elasticator.

OFFICE/CUSTOMER SERVICE

(suit starter). We are a manufacturing co based in Takanini looking for a full time office person to join our friendly team. If you are well presented, have an excell phone manner, and are familiar with MS Word, Excell, We would like to hear from you. Sense of humour essential.

PANELBEATER

Required for long established North Shore panelbeating and car painting business. Good wages and conditions. Must be well skilled and experienced.

MECHANIC

Busy Glenfield workshop requires additional mechanic. Peugeot or European exper pref but not essential. Excell cond's, friendly team, brand new premises.

MAC OPERATOR

City. Excellent opportunity to join this well known ad agency, having 2 years some experience, with catalogue work using Quark. Friendly team, great co! $35-$40K

PLUMBER / GAS FITTER Must

hold current NZ reg and preferably craftsman's gas fitter certificate, good renumerations with O/T avail.

Some ski resort hotels
Holiday Inn, Queenstown. Tel: 64-3-442 6600.
Southern Cross Ski Hotel, Canterbury. Tel: 64-3-302 8464.
Mount Hutt Country Club, Canterbury. Tel: 64-3-302 8721.
Pembroke Inn, Wanaka, Central Otago. Phone 64-3-433 7296.
Edgewater Resort, Wanaka, Central Otago. Tel: 64-3-433 8311.
Shotover Resort Hotel, Queenstown. Tel: 64-3-442 7850.
Quality Hotel, Queenstown. Tel: 64-3-442 8123.
The Queenstown Parkroyal, Queenstown. Tel: 64-3-442 7750.

Info-technology
Andrews Partners, Level 15 Quay Towers, Auckland. Tel: 64-9-373 2333.
Acorn International Ltd, Box 105-355, Auckland. Tel: 64-9-309 9043.

Engineering/technical/chemical/scientific
A-Trade NZ, 78 Worcester St, Christchurch. Tel: 64-3-365 557.
NZ Tariff & Fuel Consultants, Box 37607, Auckland. Tel: 64-9-307 6645.
Holmes Consulting Group, Box 99-450, Newmarket Auckland.

Finance & accounting specialists
Express Management & Accounting Services, Box 35 627, Auckland. Tel: 64-9-479 7325.
Johnson, David, Box 6015, Wellington. Tel: 64-4-473 4934.

General
Drake International, Box 10063, Wellington. Tel: 64-4-472 6972.
Drake International, Box 13275, Tauranga. Tel: 64-7-571 0283.
Drake International, Box 10036, Hutt City. Tel: 64-4-569 8876.
Lampen Group Ltd, 191 Queen St, Auckland. Tel: 64-9-357 9800.
Lampen, Box 2155, Wellington. Tel: 64-4-472 4157.
Advanced Personnel Services, 829 Colombo St, Box 21348, Christchurch. Tel: 64-3-365 4322.
Advanced Personnel Services, 611 Great South Rd, Manukau Central, Auckland 1701. Tel: 64-9-263 4322.

Farming
Marvin Farm Services, Box 248, Matamata 2271, Waikato. Tel: 64-7-888 6025.
Federated Farmers of NZ, Box 282, Wanganui 5015. Tel: 64-6-345 4172.

Marvin Farm Services has been running a very successful relief farming programme for over 20 years. It is, however, only available to UK residents. It would be preferable if you were over 20 years of age, and you must have had two years' dairy farm experience. Barry Hazlehurst would be very happy to answer any queries, or give you any further information you may require.

He told me that anyone who can arrange their own immigration procedures, and qualify for entry into New Zealand, would be very welcome.

We recently had a sad case here, where a group of young willing people came out on a farming contract to work for a while. They were duly taken to the farm, which was in the far north of the country, quite isolated from any main city, only to find that Immigration ordered them back to England again, without their even having seen any of New Zealand, because their documentation was incorrect. They had apparently come out on a scheme arranged by some organisation in England. It really is *very* important that you ensure that if you are coming here on a working holiday, or even coming here to live, you check out that you qualify. *Don't* take anyone else's word for it, except perhaps the Immigration officials. It is costly and heartbreaking too. Remember, there are no short cuts, and don't let anyone tell you there are.

Teaching
Responsibility for assessing the qualifications of teachers trained overseas and for decisions as to their eligibility to teach in New Zealand state schools rests with the **New Zealand Qualifications Authority** (NZQA) and the **Teacher Registration Board** (TRB). Although teachers do not need to be registered, the New Zealand Immigration Service requires that immigrants wishing to teach in New Zealand meet the criteria for registration. Information on registration requirements and fees can be obtained from the **Ministry of Education**, PO Box 1666, Wellington, NZ. Tel: 64-0800-622 222 or 64-4-473 5544. Website: *www.teachnz.govt.nz*.

A fee for assessment of qualifications is charged by the NZQA. For more information contact: Support Officer, Qualifications Evaluation Service, New Zealand Qualifications Authority, PO Box 160, Wellington 6015, New Zealand. Tel: 64-4-802 3099. Fax: 64-4-802 3401. Website: *www.nzqa.govt.nz*.

Teaching positions are advertised in the *New Zealand Education*

Gazette. Short term teaching positions are usually advertised in local newspapers. The *Education Gazette* is available by writing to PO Box 249, Wellington, New Zealand. Tel: 64-4-917 3990. Fax: 64-4-917 3991. E-mail: *vacancies@edgazette.govt.nz.* Applications and enquires concerning the positions advertised in the *Education Gazette* should be made directly to the schools concerned.

Tutoring positions at polytechnics are also advertised in the *Education Gazette* and newspapers. University teaching positions are advertised in New Zealand and overseas newspapers and periodicals.

Medical

Nursing vacancies are usually advertised in the newspapers by the relevant hospital (Crown Health Enterprise). For further information regarding employment opportunities contact:

Nursing Council Ltd, Box 9644, 97 Courtenay Place,Wellington. Tel: 64-4-385 9589. Fax: 64-4-801 8502.

The address of some private nursing agencies:

Nightingale Nurses Ltd. Box 54 137, Plimmerton, Wellington. Tel: 64-4-239 9230.
Duty Calls Nursing & Home Care Ltd, PO Box 10 270, Wellington. Tel: 64-4-499 1777.
The Christchurch Nursing Bureau Ltd, Box 3957, Christchurch. Tel: 64-3-379 9732.

Doctors

The first step that you will need to take is to confirm your eligibility for registration as a doctor in New Zealand. All matters to do with registration and examination are administered by the **Medical Council of New Zealand**. Box 156, Wellington, NZ. Tel: 64-4-472 4741. Fax: 64-4-471 0838. E-mail: *nzma@namz.org.nz.* Contact should be made before you make any applications for employment.

Most vacancies for doctors are advertised in the *New Zealand Medical Journal* which is published by the New Zealand Medical Association (NZMA). Subscription to the *New Zealand Medical Journal* is free and automatic to NZMA members. A private subscription is available and NZMA offer a special subscription service for people only interested in the classified section.

Cost of the subscription within New Zealand starts from $255.15 and outside New Zealand from $280.00 – the cost depends on the type of postage used and where in the world the *Journal* is being sent to.

The New Zealand Medical Association regret to advise that they do not retain details of medical specialist training courses in New Zealand. You will need to obtain details about this type of training from either the Medical Council or the specialist medical colleges.

New Zealand Medical Association, 26 The Terrace, PO Box 156, Wellington. Tel: 64-4-472 4741. Fax: 64-4-471 0838. E-mail: *nzma@namz.org.nz.*

Royal College of General Practitioners, Level three, 88 The Terrace, Wellington, PO Box 10440, Wellington. Tel: 64-4-496 5997. Fax: 64-4-496 5997.

Royal Australasian College of Physicians, PO Box 1634, Milton, QLD 4064. Tel: 61-7-3870 2505 Fax: 61-7-3870 2438.

Royal Australasian College of Surgeons, Surgeons Gardens, Spring Street, Melbourne, Victoria 3000, Melbourne. Tel: 61-3-9249-1273. Fax: 61-3-9249 1219.

The New Zealand Medical Association advises that the employment situation for junior doctors in New Zealand is not very promising at the moment. Local medical schools are producing more graduates than the Area Health Boards can accept, and opportunities in general practice are rather limited by the intense competition that now exists in many cities. Should you decide to move to New Zealand and take up a position as a medical practitioner, the New Zealand Medical Association would welcome your application for membership.

The following locum agencies arrange partnerships and sale of practices:

Auckland Medical Bureau, 1A Dilworth Terrace, Parnell, Auckland 1001. Tel: 64-9-377 5903.

Medical Personnel Ltd, 387 Mt Eden Road, Mt Eden, Auckland 1003, PO Box 67-003, Mt Eden. Tel: 64-9-630 1963.

SETTING UP A BUSINESS

Finding the right type of business can take time. Looking in the papers or/and contacting a real estate firm are the first steps to be taken. Write off for copies of New Zealand newspapers – see this

BUSINESS OPPORTUNITIES

NEW ZEALAND has a wide range of businesses available for lease or sale. All fields are covered and they come in various sizes as well. Some, such as motels and dairies, often include owner's accommodation. Prices vary but generally relate to returns. A sample of the current market:

NORTHERN

North Shore - Restaurant, nets $107,000, includes accom. $160,000.

Auckland – Panmure bakery, t/o $6000 weekly, good lease, good location. $120,000.

Auckland – Pukekohe day care centre, well estab. licensed for 25 2-5 year olds per day, included 3-bed. bungalow. $420,000.

Auckland – Owner-driver delivery run 3-tonne truck. approx. 2 days a week. $35,000.

Auckland – Queen St retail. 3 x 3 lease, profitable business sells to tourists and locals alike. Going concern $225,000.

Auckland – Printing business, letter press, off set and digital printing. Long est. $360,000.

Auckland – Indian takeaway, could convert to Chinese. Nice location. $29,000.

Rotorua – Superette, big shop, good location, sales $27,000 weekly. Asking $280,000 plus s.a.v.

Waikato – Near Hamilton, boarding kennels and cattery, accom. for about 30 animals. Redec. home. $295,000.

Bay of Plenty – Motel, leasehold, 19 immaculately presented units. 4-bed. accom. Leasehold $660,000.

King Country – Auto repairs, 2-bay workshop, stable business netting $70,000. $92,000.

CENTRAL

Hawke's Bay - Backpackers hostel, NZ top 10-rated. $220,000.

Wanganui – Motels, nine units, freehold going concern, excellent clientele, extra land. $720,000.

Bulls - Dairy/grocery/tackle shop. Busy intersection, local plus tourist trade, near busy airbase. $98,000 plus s.a.v.

New Plymouth - Grocery mini market, good results, great lifestyle. $79,000 plus s.a.v.

Wellington - Cafe, Tinakori Rd, excellent set-up, consistent turnover. $50,000 plus s.a.v.

Hutt Valley - Service station, busy frontage. $43,500 plus s.a.v. (about $55,000).

Wellington - Franchise, Budget Travel. Be your own boss and enjoy a new career. Market leader, strong national brand, existing business. Minimum entry level $120,000.

Wellington - Charcoal chicken takeaways, possibilities to expand into other foods, 5 days a week, cheap rent. $42,000 plus s.a.v.

SOUTHERN

Nelson - Appliance centre, repair and retail. Excellent returns. $64,000 plus s.a.v.

Christchurch - Importing/ wholesale business, established 7 years. Turnover $1 million. Top range products, good sole distribution rights. $379,000.

Christchurch - Tavern, harbour and hills outlook, seo. 3 bed. house. Excellent profitability. $490,000.

Christchurch - boarding kennels and cattery. Going concern, licensed for 120 dogs and 60 cats. Close to city centre, 3 bed. accommodation. Real potential. $170,000.

Christchurch - Fitness hire and retail, progressive business in excellent suburb. $59,500 plus stock and van.

Canterbury - Contracting, 6 machine operation in developing rural area. Too reputation, plant in great order and extra busy. $225,000.

Dunedin - Backpackers Lodge, newly est. Net operating profit $59,000 in first year. Wonderful lifestyle, great lease. $135,000.

Dunedin - Bakery, busy retail unit in good location. Turning over $5500 a week. Offers plus $43,000 stock and plant.

Wanaka - Cafe and ice creamery, prime lakefront location. Sound investment. $160,000 plus plant and stock.

Fig. 12. Some typical business opportunities for sale.

chapter for addresses.

The Small Business Agency

The Small Business Agency runs workshops to help people who wish to run their own business. These come under the headings:

- Preparation
- Making a Start
- Management and Control
- Finance.

The addresses for enquiries are:

Small Business Agency (National Office), PO Box 11-012, Wellington. Tel: 64-4-472 3141. Fax: 64-4-546 8075.

Small Business Agency, Box 609, Whangarei. Tel: 64-09-438 2515.
Bizinfo, freephone: 64-0800 424946.

If you prefer to find empty premises and start up your own business, you should contact the real estate companies. Here is a small sample of shop and office space:

- Quality Office Space, Auckland City, 7,000 square feet ground floor modern fit out, $5.50 per square foot.
- Auckland City fringe office, studio 2 car parks, 1,050 square feet, $460 per week not including goods and services tax.
- Auckland City Office in the heart of the CBD – whole floor, 4,182 square feet. Large reception, fully partitioned, $11.50 per square foot.
- Quality serviced and furnished offices – central Auckland $450 per month.
- Auckland suburb, 4,673 square feet, high stud warehouse, 2 roller doors, $5.50 per square foot.
- Auckland suburb, 8,100 square feet of manufacturing space, 16 carparks, $5,500 per annum.
- Auckland City fringe live in/work 3,600 square feet office/ showroom/accommodation.
- Auckland fringe showroom, 2,081 square feet, $29800 per annum.

Farming as a business

Pastoral agriculture is practised throughout New Zealand, with beef cattle predominating in the far north, dairying in Waikato (central North Island) and Taranaki (lower North Island), and sheep

MASTERTON RURAL — $170,000 + GST
Low Maintenance Living
125 acres, flat to medium hill. Country style 3 brm home, located 22 mins from town.

GREYTOWN RURAL — $100,000 (NO GST)
5.0156 Ha 12.4 Acres
5 paddocks, 2 bay implement shed with power. Own water supply, shelter planted. Rural rates.

WAIHI 1800 sqft Canadian log home on 5 acres, 3km to town. 4 bedrooms, log dble garage with sleepout, double carport, 6000 sqft shed, stream and rural outlook. $230,000.

LAND: THE INVESTMENT OF THE FUTURE. Four good quality soil type rural blocks. Power is laid on and fresh water stream flows through part of the subdivision. Lots 1 & 4 approx 3 acres $62,000 and $57,000. Lots 3 14½ acres $145,000. Lot 2 12½ acres $120,000.

MASTERTON Forestry Blocks available now. 318 acres (128ha), some scrub and grazing, 70km Masterton, $60,000 + GST. 410 acre (166ha), medium hill, 20% grazeable scrub, $150,000 + GST. 88ha, 217 acres, medium hill, 40% grazeable scrub, rest clear, $85,000 + GST. 50ha (123 acres) medium hill, 20% light scrub, no gorse, $65,000 + GST. 28ha (69 acres) medium to steeper hill, clear $45,000

BEEF OR DEER FATTENING UNIT
1 acres of easy rolling contour in a top farming location. Well subdivided into 7 main deer fenced paddocks, 2 holding paddocks, good deer facilities, cattle and sheep yards, large implement shed and hay barn. Situated on both school bus routes within 10 mintues of Waipukurau this sunny, northerly facing home enjoys lovely views. Well worth your inspection at $228,000 + GST

NELSON FARMLET — $180,000
4 ha (10 acres) 15 minutes t Richmond
Spectacular 360° views
Horse dressage ring
3 brm home, double garage workshop
Close to beach

WAIKANAE: $389,000. *$30,000 Below GV* Excellent home, brick exterior, concrete floor, decromastic roof, double internal garage. 3 bedrooms, separate lounge, family room or games room. Beautiful gardens, trees. 5.10ha (12.6 acres), glasshouse, outbuildings etc.

Fig. 13. Some typical farming enterprises for sale.

farming in the hills and in the south of the North Island. In the South Island, sheep farming is the main form of pastoral agriculture, with a sprinkling of beef cattle farmed in the high and hill country and wetter flat areas, and some dairying on the flat land of both coasts.

Livestock is rarely housed, but feeding of small quantities of supplements such as hay and silage can occur, particularly in winter. Grass growth is seasonal, largely depending on location and climatic fluctuations, but normally occurs for between eight and twelve months of the year. Stock is grazed in paddocks, often with movable electric fences, which allow rotation of grazing around the farm. Lambing and calving are carefully managed to take full advantage of spring grass growth.

For further information on farms and farming in New Zealand, contact:

New Zealand Dairy Board, Pastoral House, 25 The Terrace, Box 417, Wellington. Tel: 64-4-471 8300. Fax: 64-4-471 8600. Website: *www.nzmilk.co.nz*.

Meat Producers Board, Wellington. Tel: 64-4-473 9150.

Wools of New Zealand, Box 3225, Wellington. Tel: 64-4-472 6888. Fax: 64-4-473 7872. Website: *www.maf.govt.nz*.

New Zealand Dairy Board, Private Bag 1992, Christchurch. Tel: 64-3-366 8416.

PAYING TAX IN NEW ZEALAND

Income tax is imposed by the New Zealand Government on income derived by a taxpayer in each income year. The tax year runs from 1 April to 31 March. The adoption of a balance date other than 31 March is approved where the business cycle makes it appropriate, or conformity with overseas balance dates is required, but the balance date is related backwards or forwards to the nearest 31 March for the purposes of applying tax legislation.

Income tax is levied and payable by every 'person' on all the income derived by that person during the income year. A 'person' is legally defined to include individuals, companies, local or public authorities and an unincorporated body of persons.

At present there is virtually no capital gains tax or wealth tax in New Zealand, but profits from certain speculative ventures and transactions in land or investments may in certain circumstances be liable to income tax.

A person, including a company, is assessable for income tax on all world-wide income derived while a resident of New Zealand. A **tax credit**, not exceeding the relevant New Zealand tax on the foreign source income, is allowed for foreign tax payable where such tax is similar in nature to New Zealand income tax.

A non-resident is assessable for income tax only on income with a source in New Zealand. Income with a source in New Zealand includes income derived from:

- any business wholly or partly carried on in New Zealand
- contracts made or performed in New Zealand
- service as an employee or agent in New Zealand
- the ownership of land in New Zealand
- investments in New Zealand companies or institutions
- money lent in New Zealand
- royalties deductible by the payer against New Zealand income.

Only in the first two instances is income apportionable between sources in New Zealand and sources overseas.

'Place of abode' test

The **permanent place of abode test** is the primary test of residence. An individual who is personally present in New Zealand for more than 183 days in total, over a 12 month period, will be deemed to be resident.

A person will be deemed not to be a resident in New Zealand where that person is personally absent for a period or periods in total of 325 days in any period of 12 months, provided that person is not resident in New Zealand by reason of maintaining a permanent place of abode in New Zealand, or is in the service of the New Zealand Government.

It is possible for a taxpayer to be resident in two countries. If this is the case, where a **double tax treaty** is in existence, the tie breaking provisions in the relevant tax treaty should be used to describe the taxpayer's residence for the purposes of the treaty.

Pay As You Earn (PAYE)

The PAYE tax deducted is not a final tax for the employee, but rather it is used to offset the employee's tax liability at the end of the year. This means that a refund (or a further tax liability) may arise.

Individuals are taxed under a progressive rate system. The rate of tax is:

- 19.5% for income not exceeding $38,000
- 33% for income between $38,001 – $60,000
- 39% for income exceeding $60,000.

Non-resident individuals are subject to non-resident **withholding tax** on interest, dividends and royalties, which in some circumstances is a final tax. On all other income from New Zealand, non-resident individuals are taxed at the same rates as residents.

Many employers pay allowances to their employees. These allowances can either be taxable or non-taxable, depending on what the allowance relates to.

An allowance paid to an employee in respect of expenditure incurred for private purposes gives rise to a benefit to the employee and is assessable as monetary remuneration, or is subject to **fringe benefit tax** and is paid in non-monetary form.

An allowance paid to an employee as a reimbursement of expenses incurred by the employee on behalf of the employer is not a benefit to the employee and is therefore not assessable.

Resident companies are taxed at a flat rate of 33 cents in the dollar, while non-resident companies are taxed at a flat and final tax of 38 cents in the dollar.

PAYE deduction tables
Here is an extract from the weekly tax tables to give you some idea of the deductions you can expect from your weekly paypacket. Accident Compensation deductions are included.

Earnings	Tax payable (approx.)
$200	$33.63
$250	$44.78
$300	$55.93
$350	$67.08
$400	$78.23
$430	$84.92
$460	$91.61
$480	$96.07
$500	$100.53
$520	$104.99
$530	$107.22
$540	$109.45
$550	$111.68
$560	$113.91

$580	$118.37
$600	$122.83
$650	$133.98
$700	$145.13

Further advice and information

For **company tax, withholding tax, provisional tax** and any other information you may be interested in, you could contact one of the Peat Marwick offices, where you will be able to update any information you already have, and receive advice on any areas which are of particular interest to you:

KPMG Peat Marwick New Zealand Offices:
PO Box 1584, 9 Princess Street, Auckland. Tel: 64-9-367 5800.
Hamilton. Tel: 64-7-858 6500.
Wellington. Tel: 64-4-382 8800.
Website: *www.kpmg.co.nz*.

BANKING AND FINANCE

Registered banks dominate the New Zealand financial system. The registration of banks in New Zealand is governed by the **Reserve Bank of New Zealand Act 1989**. This gives the Reserve Bank of New Zealand authority to register institutions providing certain criteria are met.

International banks operate as registered banks in New Zealand, either as a locally incorporated company registered bank or a branch of the parent bank.

Overview of banking

Ultimate control of banking in New Zealand lies with the Reserve Bank of New Zealand. There are three categories of financial institutions which operate within New Zealand:

Registered banks
Most large financial institutions are registered banks. The registered banks are subject to the Reserve Bank's prudential supervision requirements. Their activities can vary from the provision of full retail and wholesale banking services, to specialised niche banking areas.

Savings banks
The traditional role of savings banks has been directed towards the collection of household savings and the provision of long-term finance on the security of residential property. The deregulation of the New Zealand banking system, which permits registered banks to undertake the functions previously performed exclusively by savings banks, has resulted in very few financial institutions being left in this category.

Other financial institutions
These consist of merchant banks and finance companies. Merchant banks operate primarily in the wholesale market and offer a wide range of financial services to corporate clients. This includes the management of investment portfolios, treasury management, underwriting of securities and advice on mergers and acquisitions. Finance companies lend primarily to individuals and businesses with security over assets purchased with the funding. Finance company receivables include consumer credit, leasing, floor plan and finance for real estate development. Finance company facilities are generally short to medium term and at fixed interest rates.

The Reserve Bank of New Zealand (RBNZ)
The RBNZ acts as the central bank for New Zealand. As central bank the Reserve Bank is not acting in competition with the commercial banks. Its duties lie in overseeing the activities of the NZ financial markets.

The Reserve Bank's primary functions include:

- managing the money supply through the issue of Reserve Bank bills
- bank registration and prudential supervision of banks
- implementing the Government's monetary policy to achieve and maintain price stability
- providing banking services to the Government, other public sector entities, settlement banks and overseas central banks
- managing the foreign exchange rate
- advising the Government and other appropriate bodies on economic policy
- acting as Registrar for Government stock.

New Zealand banks
New Zealand no longer has total ownership of any bank. The main

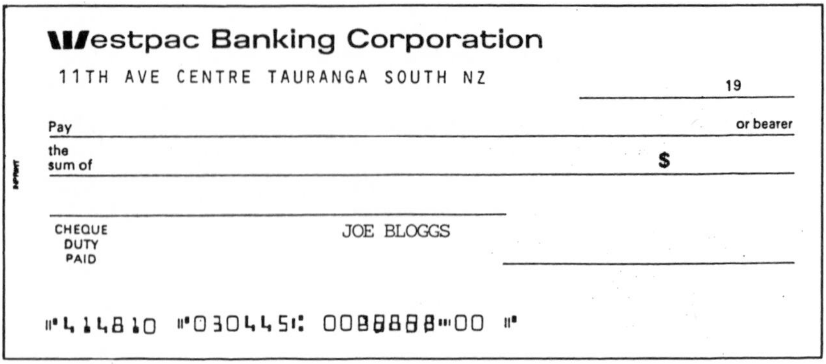

Fig. 14. A New Zealand bank cheque.

ownership is Australian with Australia New Zealand Bank, Bank of New Zealand, National Australia Bank (NZ) Ltd and Westpac Banking Corporation. The National Bank of New Zealand is British owned.

New Zealand currency

The decimal currency system was introduced in 1967. The New Zealand dollar became the monetary unit, replacing the pounds, shillings and pence system. We have $1 and $2 coins, $5, $10, $20, $50 and $100 dollar notes.

QUESTIONS AND ANSWERS

What does the Double Tax Treaty allow?

New Zealand has agreements for the avoidance of double taxation with 24 countries. The basic principle is that the country of source has the prior right to tax; the country of residence provides either a tax exemption or a tax credit.

Is the rental of property taxable?

Yes. Interest, rents and royalties form part of an individual taxpayer's income and will be assessed at the full rates. Individuals who are subject to PAYE (Pay As You Earn) may also be liable to make provisional tax payments if their residual income tax in relation to income other than source deduction payments exceeds $2,500 in an income year.

4

Education

EDUCATIONAL REFORM

In 1987 the then Government, the Labour Party, led by David Lange as Prime Minister and self appointed Minister of Education, named a task force to review education and its administration. Since then nearly every aspect of the administration of education in New Zealand has been reviewed. The task force found that structures that had been in place for over a hundred years were in need of extensive reform as they were too centralised and too complex.

The basic aim of these reforms was to improve the quality of education for all New Zealanders and their recommendations were that education should be based on choice, giving a range of options to both pupils and the institutions that provide education. The wishes and aims of parents and those in any education community needed to be recognised, and education needed to be culturally sensitive and provide equal opportunities and to practise good management.

THE SCHOOLS

The most significant changes were in the administration of primary and secondary schools, in partnership with teachers. Previously, this had been the responsibility of education boards and the regional offices of the Department of Education. This responsibility was now decentralised to boards of trustees of individual schools who became accountable for meeting the objectives of their **charter** (an agreement between the school and the Minister of Education). Expenditure was made from bulk grants received from Government to run education institutions. The boards of trustees are now required to report to the Education Review Office, which reviews how well schools are meeting the objectives of their charter. The Education Review Office in turn reports directly to the Minister of Education.

Starting age

Most New Zealand students start their education at the age of five years, despite the legal starting age of six years. In 1990 100 per cent of five year olds were in fact enrolled at primary school.

It will help your child integrate into the new school if you as parents make an effort to become involved. School camps, for example, take place in the summer months. The children, teachers and helpers spend 3–4 days away together at a camp, sometimes in the bush, in a relaxed situation, learning new skills. Parents are always needed to help out, in the kitchens preparing food, and also being involved in the various activities. It gives a greater understanding of the different roles the teacher is required to play.

Consider joining your own School Board of Trustees, and become involved with the committees when asked. There is no better way for you and your family to become familiar with the new life style. I found that I made most of my friends from amongst the other parents I met at socials organised by the School Parent Teacher Association, and they still remain friends even though our families are now grown up.

The school curriculum

Primary/intermediate

In primary and intermediate schools the curriculum subjects cover oral and written language, reading, writing and spelling, mathematics, social studies, science, art and craft, physical and health education and music.

Intermediate school

At intermediate school the curriculum covers (in addition to the primary school curriculum) the skills of woodwork, metalwork, cooking and sewing.

Junior classes

The first three years of the child's education is spent in junior classes (Junior 1–3). Promotion is by age through the Standards 1–4 classes, and continues through Forms One and Two.

Secondary schools

Most secondary schools cater for students from Form Three to Form Seven, with average ages ranging from 13–18 years. Attendance is now compulsory until the age of 16, and education is provided free to the age of 19 years. The **core curriculum** subjects for secondary schools for Form Three to Form Four are language, social studies, mathematics, general science, health and physical education, music, art and craft, home economics. Optional subjects may include economics, history, geography, French, Japanese and German. At Form Five to Form Seven levels, students have a wide range of subjects to choose from.

Old school tie
The old school tie attitude is still alive and well in some New Zealand private schools, despite the protests from those whose education was gained at the expense of the State system.

Private schools
Most of the private schools in New Zealand, even those previously well known and respected for their religious independence, have became part of the state education system by integration.

There are, however, still some registered private primary and secondary schools run by religious to philosophical organisations or private individuals. These schools aim to provide education that places more emphasis on religious beliefs, skills, attitudes and values.

Parents are prepared to pay for the right to educate their children in the way they believe. This attitude is not only related to religion, but also to academic and behavioural values.

Boarding schools
In New Zealand, attendance at a boarding school is not necessarily just for the rich. Because of the large rural communities, who quite often live in very isolated areas, many parents choose to send their children to boarding schools, partly for the standard of education but also because of the need for their children to socialise. Most boarding schools also accept day pupils.

Dilworth School
A past Labour Party leader, Mike Moore, was educated at Dilworth School in Auckland. This school was founded under the terms of the will of James Dilworth. The trust deed requires 'that pupils be orphans or the sons of persons of good character and in straited circumstances'.

Correspondence School
This national school provides distance education for pre-schoolers,

full-time primary and secondary pupils doing one or more subjects, and adult full-time or part-time students who wish to continue their education. For further information on this form of education see the addresses at the back of this book.

Polynesian schools

Auckland is regarded now as the Polynesian capital of the world, and understandably, many schools in the Auckland area are either totally Polynesian or have a large percentage of Polynesian pupils. This means that many of the education programmes are orientated towards Polynesian culture and standards are modified to allow for language difficulties. Maori language and culture is taught widely in all New Zealand schools.

Latest education developments

A recent Minister of Education, Lockwood Smith, proposed a curriculum structure that established the essential learning areas, the skills needed and the values young children should learn at school. It set out the compulsory requirements from new entrants to school leavers.

The essential areas of learning are language, maths, science, technology, social sciences, the arts, health and physical well being.

It was intended also to reinforce the values of individual and collective responsibility of honesty, reliability, respect for others and for the law, tolerance, fairness, caring and compassion, non-sexism and non-racism.

Secondary school attainments

School Certificate
The School Certificate examination is taken by most pupils at the end of three years of secondary education. Except for part-time adult students, each candidate's course of study must include English, although the student is not required to sit the examination in that subject. A candidate may enter the examination in any number of subjects up to six and is credited with a grade for each subject. These are seven grades – A1 (highest), A2, B1, B2 (middle), C1, C2, and D (lowest).

School Certificate is broadly equivalent to the UK General Certificate of Secondary Education (GCSE) at grades A–E; the UK General Certificate in Education (GCE) at O level; the UK Certificate of Secondary Education (CSE) at grades one to three; and the Canadian or United States Grade 10.

Sixth Form Certificate
Sixth Form Certificate is awarded, on a single-subject basis to pupils who have satisfactorily completed a course of one year in one or more subjects. No more than six subjects can be taken. Each school candidate must study a course of English, though the candidate is not required to enter it as a Sixth Form Certificate qualification. Grades are awarded on a 1–9 scale, grade one being the highest.

Sixth Form Certificate is broadly equivalent to Canadian or United States Grade 11.

Higher School Certificate
Higher School Certificate is awarded to pupils who have been accepted for entry to Form Six and have since satisfactorily completed an advanced course of two years in at least three subjects. It is also awarded to pupils who have obtained an 'A' or 'B' Bursary qualification from the University Bursaries Examination.

Higher School Certificate, University Bursary or University Scholarship is broadly equivalent to UK GCE A levels; Canadian or United States Grade 12; in different Australian States, per 12 awards, Higher School Certificate, Senior Certificate, Matriculation, and Secondary School Certificate.

Bursary and scholarship examinations
The **University Bursaries Examination** is usually taken by secondary school pupils in Form Seven. It is a competitive examination for supplementary awards for study at a university. Subject scholarships are awarded on the basis of results in this examination and are administered by the New Zealand Qualifications Authority.

POLYTECHNIC EDUCATION

Since the early 1980s vocational education and training has moved away from the secondary to the continuing education sector. Training formerly provided by technical high schools is now provided by polytechnics. Disciplines cover career choices such as Tourism and Hospitality, Art and Design, Fishing and Marine, Agriculture, Business, Engineering, Building and Construction and Science and Technology. There are 25 polytechnics in New Zealand; the addresses for the main ones are at the back of the book. Contact the Association of Polytechnics in NZ in Auckland on Tel: 64-9-849 4180, fax: 64-9-815 2901, for further information.

Approximate Secondary Education Costs

Tuition fees	$	Per year $
State High School		120.00
Catholic School		8,500.00
Private School		16,325.00
– Registration fee	175.00	
– Enrolment fee	562.50	17,062.00
Boarding School		7,560.00
Exam fees – Form Five, five papers		75.00
– Form Seven, five papers		165.00

Sports gear	
Sports uniform	65.00
Tennis racquet	200.00
Cricket bat	200.00
Hockey stick	200.00

Incidentals	
Travel	500.00
Lunches	720.00
School trips	200.00

School clothing	
Boy's basic per year	650.00
Blazer	147.00
Girl's basic per year	700.00
Blazer	140.00

Requisites	
Stationery	80.00
Arts and craft	25.00
Schoolbag	50.00

Extras	
Private music tuition one hour per week for 32 weeks	1,000.00
Music lesson half hour per week for 32 weeks	800.00
Instrument hire	200.00

Sports coaching	
Tennis one hour per week for 32 weeks	1,200.00
Swimming one hour per week for 32 weeks	320.00

COSTS OF EDUCATION

Educating children can be costly, especially if they go to private school and then to university. Some estimates suggest it would cost $132,927 to send a girl to private secondary school, independent boarding school, and to medical school. Five years' boarding is about $37,800 plus five years at a private school is around $81,625 and medical school is about $13,496 per year. Some sources suggest the costs could top $200,000 to become a doctor and as much as $50,000 to complete a Bachelor of Arts degree.

UNIVERSITIES OF NEW ZEALAND

New Zealand has seven universities: the University of Auckland, University of Waikato (Hamilton), Massey University (Palmerston Worth), Victoria University of Wellington, University of Canterbury (Christchurch), Lincoln University (Christchurch) and University of Otago (Dunedin).

All the universities offer courses in a wide range of subjects in the arts, social sciences, commerce and science. Law and music courses are available at Auckland, Victoria, Canterbury and Otago universities. Most universities specialist in certain fields.

- The University of Otago offers courses in medicine, dentistry, surveying, home science, physical education and pharmacy.

- The University of Canterbury offers courses in forestry, engineering and fine arts.

- Lincoln University specialises in agriculture and horticulture and offers a wide range of commerce courses.

- The University of Auckland offers courses in architecture, planning, engineering, medicine, optometry and fine arts.

- Victoria University offers courses in architecture, public administration and social work.

- Massey University has courses in agriculture, horticulture, food technology and veterinary science as well as extramural tuition in a wide range of subjects for students.

Each university sets its own programmes, and each university council sets the dates for terms or semesters. All matters relating to management are the responsibility of the council of the institution

INITIAL APPLICATION FORM FOR A PLACE AT A NEW ZEALAND SCHOOL,
POLYTECHNIC OR COLLEGE OF EDUCATION

THE PRINCIPAL

_____
(Name of Institution)

_____
(Address)
NEW ZEALAND

Dear Sir/Madam
I would like to study in New Zealand and should be grateful if you could:

a   allot me a place at your institution for_____
                          (**state year and form or programme in which you wish to study**)
b   advise whether you are able to arrange hostel accommodation, private board, or a place in a student flat
(indicate preference or delete if making your own arrangements for accommodation).
My personal details are as follows:

Name: _____
          (Family   name)   (Personal names)
Address:_____

Telephone number: _____   Subjects being studied this year (indicate
                                            which subjects are taught in English):
Date of birth: _____   _____

Sex: _____   _____

Citizenship_____   _____
                                            I have made arrangements for accommodation
Present school and class: _____   with the following host (state if no accommo-
                                            dation arranged).

_____   _____

_____   _____
Previous Schools attended: I would like to study the following subjects at your
_____   institution (for secondary school students only)

_____   _____

First Language: _____   _____
                                            When I leave secondary school I intend to study
Number of years studying English: _____   further for (state the qualifications aimed at, e.g.
                                            Bachelor of Arts):
Examination results (attach certified copies _____
of certificates for any public English tests
attempted and ALL public and school exam-
inations taken in the two previous years): _____
_____   I attach a testimonial from the principal of my
                                            present school (to include comments on general
          ability, competence in English and ability to adjust
_____   to a new environment).

(Applicant's signature)_____   (Date) _____

Fig. 15. Applying for a place in education.

which represents the interest of staff, students and the community. The council is also responsible for approving course regulations and for maintaining the equivalences of courses for degrees and other qualifications.

The university academic year runs from late February to early November each year. A university education is open to anyone meeting the entry criteria set by the individual universities.

Choosing the right university

It can be very difficult to assess which university would be the right one for you when you are living overseas, so here is a brief description of all seven to help you with this decision. The fees are for the 2000 year, so it would be advisable to check they have not changed when you make your enquiries at the university of your choice.

When you have been accepted by the university of your choice you will automatically be passed on to the correct department for accommodation to be arranged.

Auckland University

The University of Auckland opened in 1883 and is the largest of New Zealand's seven universities. The University is in the centre of Auckland City, separated from the tower blocks of the central business district by historic Albert Park, where students can sit and relax in between lectures. To the south east lie the trees and open spaces of the Auckland Domain.

The proximity of the University to the cultural and commercial amenities of New Zealand's largest city, attractive green setting and harbour views, bestow advantages enjoyed by few inner city campuses anywhere.

Student accommodation
University halls of residence are available from NZ$150 to $185 per week, including two meals per day, but many students prefer to share private flats or houses, and there is a large selection of rented accommodation available at reasonable rates. Here students can expect to pay NZ$87 to $150 per week, plus a share of the food, telephone and electricity costs.

For further information contact the Accommodation and Conference Centre, 14–16 Mount Street, Auckland. Tel: 64-9-373 7599 ext 7691. Fax: 64-9-373 7552. Website: *www.auckland.ac.nz*.Or Auckland University International Office at Private Bag 92019. Tel: 64-9-373 7513. Fax: 64-9-373 7405. E-mail: *international@auckland.ac.nz*.

Auckland University: Approximate International Student Fees

Degree	No. of years	Tuition fee NZ$
Faculty of Architecture		
Bachelor of Architecture Studies (BAS)	3	17,500
Bachelor of Architecture Studies (BArch)	2	17,500
Bachelor of Property (BProp)	3	12,500
Bachelor of Planning (BPlan)	4	15,000
Faculty of Arts		
Humanities – non laboratory based	minimum of 3	10,000
Social Sciences, Languages	minimum of 3	12,500
Performance, Geography, Psychology	minimum of 3	15,000
Faculty of Commerce		
Bachelor of Commerce (BCom)	minimum of 3	12,500
Faculty of Engineering		
Bachelor of Engineering (BE)	4	17,500
Faculty of Fine Art		
Bachelor of Fine Art (BFA)	4	15,000
Faculty of Law		
Bachelor of Law (LLB)	4	–
Law 1 (Legal System course for law intermediate)	–	see notes
Law 2 (Years 2-4)	–	12,500

Notes:
An LLB is made up two parts; Part 1 is made up of the Legal Systems paper and a variety of other subjects from the university's general degree programmes. The cost for the first year therefore depends on the choice of papers from the supporting degree. Part 2 only starts if the student has been admitted into this stage; the selection is based on academic merit.

Degree	No. of years	Tuition fee NZ$
Faculty of Music		
Bachelor of Music – Performance (BMus)	3	15,000
Faculty of Science		
Bachelor of Science (BSc)		
– Math, Computing, Information Science	3	12,500
– Other	3	15,000
Auckland Consortium for Theological Education (ACTE)		
Bachelor of Theology (BTheol)	3	10,000
Interfaculty Degree		
Bachelor of Technology	4	Yr 1-3 15,000
		Yr 4 17,500

Conjoint Degrees
In addition to the above listed single degrees it is possible to combine some of them.

Postgraduate courses
The Auckland University offers a wide range of postgraduate degrees and diplomas. For further information contact the International Office, University of Auckland, PO Box 92019, Auckland.
E-mail: *international@auckland.ac.nz*

Fig. 16. Auckland University tuition fees.

Lincoln University

Lincoln first opened its doors to students in 1878 as a small school of agriculture. A few years later Lincoln become Canterbury Agricultural College and a degree course in agriculture was added to the curriculum.

In 1961, Lincoln became a University College with close ties to the University of Canterbury and in 1990 it received independent university status. Lincoln University thus became New Zealand's seventh and newest university.

The University is situated in rural surroundings, 20km from Christchurch. The township of Lincoln is close by, and has a good range of shops and services.

Lincoln now offers a wide range of single or multi-disciplinary research opportunities and has a tradition of commitment to postgraduate students at Lincoln University. Staff have expertise in the supervision and management of postgraduate programmes in commerce and management, primary production and natural resources, science and technology, and social sciences.

Close links with resource-based industries, government and private organisations and other bodies ensure that Lincoln University research programmes are relevant to society's needs. Students may receive advice and some supervision from skilled people employed by other organisations, and funding is available sometimes for collaborative programmes.

Farms

The University has five farms, as well as an orchard and a Horticultural Research Unit. The Research, Dairy and Arable Farms, together with the Horticultural Research Unit and the Sheep Breeding Unit, are adjacent to the campus.

Most field research work is done on the Research Farm and the Horticultural Research Area, but larger farm trials are carried out on the other units. Land and animals for research are allocated by a committee so that, as far as possible, every request is adequately accommodated.

Student accommodation

Accommodation is available in the halls of residence at a cost about $168 per week – this includes two meals a day. Self-catering halls of residence start from $90 per week, which includes electricity, heating and telephone calls. Student flats start from $78 per week – this does not include electricity, heating and telephone calls. Family units are

---

Lincoln University: Approximate International Tuition Fees

Undergraduate Courses	NZ$
B.C.M, B.Com (Tourism), B.Com (H & I.M), B.C.M, B.Com(H)	11,500
B.Com (Tran), B.Com (VPM), B.R.S, B.Com, B.R.S, B.R.M, B.Soc	11,500
B.Com (Ag), B.Com (Forestry), B.Com (Hort)	12,000
B.Agr, B.E, B.Hort, B.L.A, B.Sc	14,500
Cert F.S, Cert Nat. Res	13,000
Cert Wool	4,875
Honours	
B.P.R & T.M, B.Soc.Sc, B.R.S	11,500
B.Com	13,500
B.Agr.Sc, B.Hort.Sc, B.Sc	14,500
Undergraduate Diplomas	
Dip.F.M, Dip.Hort.Mgt.	13,500
Postgraduate Diplomas	
P.G.Dip.Agr.Eng, P.G.Dip.AGR.Sc, P.G.Dip.Appl.Sc	15,000
P.G.Dip.Hort.Sc, P.G.Dip.Soc.Sc, P.G.Dip.V&O	15,000
Masters Degrees and PhDs	
Animal and Food Sciences	28,500
Applied Management and Computing	17,000
Commerce	13,500
Environmental Management and Design	22,000
Human Sciences	16,000
Soil, Plant and Ecological Sciences	28,500

Note: All fees are subject to change.

Fig. 17. Lincoln University tuition fees.

priced from $165 per week and also does not include electricity, heating and telephone calls. For further information contact the Accommodation Services, PO Box 84, Lincoln University, Canterbury, NZ. Tel: 64-3-325 3620. Fax: 64-3-325 2960. E-mail: *taylor@lincoln.ac.nz*.

University of Waikato, Hamilton

Waikato University was established in 1964. There are currently nearly 10,000 students enrolled, including 250 international students. The spacious and picturesque campus is situated 3km from Hamilton City. Its facilities include well-equipped modern teaching buildings and laboratories which are grouped in a central academic area on an attractively landscaped campus covering 64 hectares. The campus also boasts a new recreation centre, extensive sporting grounds and a swimming pool.

The University region is steeped in Maori history and it includes four of the major tribal confederations, Tainui, Te Arawa, Mataatua, and Tairawhiti.

Student accommodation
There are five halls of residence costing roughly $161 per week, per room – this includes three catered meals. Older students usually prefer to share a flat or house with other students, and there is a range of houses to choose from such as three- to five-bedroom houses on their own plot of land, or two-storied units/apartment blocks. You can expect to pay between $95 and $125 per week, per room; additional costs include electricity, telephone and food. For further information contact the International Students Office, University of Waikato, Private Bag 3105, Hamilton, NZ. Tel: 64-7-838 4439. Fax: 64-7-838 4269.

Otago University, Dunedin
Founded in 1869, the University of Otago is recognised internationally as a leader in many areas of research, and has first class status as a teaching institution. The campus is one of the most beautiful and closely knit in New Zealand. The waters of the Leith River meander through the grounds, which have an attractive blend of historic and modern buildings. The University is ringed by the halls of residence and these are surrounded by the distinctive Victorian and Edwardian houses and modern flats which are used for student accommodation. The University is only five minutes from the centre of Dunedin.

Student accommodation
Accommodation is available in the halls of residence at a cost of about $160 per week. Private board is also available for around $110 per week. Sharing a house or flatting on present room rates will cost about $85 per week, plus food, electricity and power. For further information regarding the University, its courses and accommodation contact Otago University at PO Box 56, Dunedin, NZ. Tel: 64-3-479 8344. Fax: 64-3-479 8367. E-mail: *international@otago.ac.nz*.

Canterbury University, Christchurch
Canterbury is located in Christchurch, the largest city in South Island. On the coastal edge of the Canterbury plains, the city is close to both the sea and mountains. Christchurch is commonly referred

University of Canterbury

Application for Admission *ad eundem statum*

1. Mr
   Mrs...
   Miss   *First name(s)*   *Surname or Family Name*
   Ms

2. (a) Date of Birth................................. (b) Place of birth................................. (c) Married or Single.................................

3. (a) Country of Citizenship... (b) Country of Permanent Residence...

4. (a) **Degree course to be taken.**... (b) **Major subject**...

5. I hereby apply for admission to the University of Canterbury *ad eundem statum: (Cross out the lines which do not apply)*

   either   (a) at entrance level

   or   (b) with credits towards the proposed degree course to be taken

   or   (c) with the status of graduate
                (Degree)... (University)...

6. **EVIDENCE:** I attach the following certificates (originals or certified copies) in support of my application.

   ....

   ....

   CERTIFIED COPIES: If copies of documents are sent, each copy must be certified as a true copy by a Justice of the Peace, Solicitor, Notary Public or an official of the institution that issued the original document and must bear the official stamp of that person. Uncertified photo copies will not be accepted.

7. **FEE:** I enclose the fee of $N.Z.60 (including G.S.T.) (or sufficient of some other currency to yield this amount)

   Method of Payment...(e.g. cheque, money order, bank draft, etc.)

8. **COMPETENCE IN ENGLISH:** If applicable, complete the appropriate section.
   I have sat IELTS/TOEFL on.................................I shall be sitting IELTS/TOEFL on...

9. **CERTIFICATE OF IDENTITY:**

   I ....
        First Name(s)   *Surname or Family Name*

   of ....
        town   *country*

   .... hereby certify that I am the person named in the certificates or statements listed above.
   (occupation)

   Dated this...Day of..19..............................

   SIGNATURE   SIGNATURE
   OF APPLICANT.. OF WITNESS...

   Address........ .... Address...

   ....

This form should be sent with the other documents to:
THE REGISTRAR, UNIVERSITY OF CANTERBURY, PRIVATE BAG 4800, CHRISTCHURCH, NEW ZEALAND.
A separate application must be made for enrolment. If your application for admission is successful you will be sent an application form.

Fig. 18. Application for admission to the University of Canterbury.

to within New Zealand as the 'Garden City' and is surrounded by beautiful parks, beaches, reserves and is renowned for its recreational and cultural facilities.

The University's modern and well-equipped facilities spread across a spacious suburban campus, close to the city centre. The campus buildings have a floor area of 155,000 square metres in a park-like setting of 76 hectares and are home to over 12,500 students. The University of Canterbury offers a wide range of subjects in a variety of flexible degree structures.

Student accommodation
First year undergraduate students will be assisted to find accommodation in private homes with New Zealand families (private board). There is no permanent university accommodation for overseas students, but it is possible to stay in the Ilam Flats for four weeks. The Manager may be able to extend this time during the period June to November to allow students time to find their own accommodation.

Only a limited number of students can be given the initial four weeks in the Ilam Flats, so early arrangements are essential. Accommodation for spouses is only available in Ilam Flats from mid-November to mid-February. It is important to apply for accommodation well in advance as you may have to wait a month or more for vacancies. To make your reservations please contact The Manager, Ilam Flats, University of Canterbury, Private Bag 4800, Christchurch. Tel: 64-3-348 3441. Bookings will only be accepted if you have been accepted for the course.

Accommodation in private board may cost in the region of NZ $160 per week. Private flats may cost up to $100 per week, depending on the number sharing the flat. This does not include food, telephone and electricity.

For further information on Canterbury University apply to the Registrar, University of Canterbury, Private Bag 4800, Christchurch. Tel: 64-3-366 7001. Fax: 64-3-364 2999.

Approximate tuition fees	Undergraduate	Postgraduate
Arts	$12,000	$15,500
Commerce	$13,000	$15,000
Science	$16,000	$18,000
Engineering	$18,500	$20,000
Forestry Science	$17,000	$20,000
Law	$13,000	$15,500

Victoria University: Approximate International Tuition Fees

Degree	No. of years	Tuition fee NZ$
Faculty of Architecture		
First Year Architecture	1	15,000
Bachelor of Architecture Studies	4	17,000
Master of Architecture Studies	1	19,500
Faculty of Arts		
Bachelor of Arts	minimum of 3	10,750
Bachelor of Arts with Honours	1	13,000
Master of Arts (Thesis)	1	13,000
Faculty of Commerce		
Bachelor of Commerce (BCA)	minimum of 3	12,000
Bachelor of Commerce with Honours	minimum of 3	15,000
Faculty of Engineering		
Bachelor of Engineering (BE)	4	12,000
Faculty of Fine Art		
Bachelor of Fine Art (BFA)	4	15,000
Faculty of Law		
Bachelor of Law (LLB)	4	11,000
Bachelor of Law with Honours	1	13,000
Master of Law	1	15,000
Diploma/ Certificate in Law	1	10,700
PhD Law	3	15,000
Faculty of Music		
Bachelor of Music	3	13,000
Bachelor of Music with Honours	1	13,000
Master of Music	1	16,500
Faculty of Science		
Bachelor of Science (BSc)	3	15,000
Bachelor of Science with Honours	1	16,500
Master of Science	2	20,000

Note: The above fees are subject to change.
For further information, Website: *www.vuw.ac.nz*.

Fig. 19. Victoria University tuition fees.

Tuition fees paid in advance of enrolment will be refunded if the student does not enrol.

Victoria University, Wellington

Victoria University is situated on an imposing 16 hectare site overlooking the capital and its harbour. It lies within easy walking distance of the city centre, which can be reached by the cable car, and the National Library and Parliament buildings (the 'Beehive').

Established in 1899 Victoria was until 1962 a College of the University of New Zealand. With a faculty structure similar to that of many British universities, it offers both traditional academic disciplines within a flexible degree structure and a range of specialist courses. Recently there has been a major expansion in areas such as management, marketing and information systems, Asian and Pacific languages, Maori studies, English as a foreign language, drama, public and social policy and criminology.

The campus provides opportunities to take part in a variety of activities, as well as welfare and support services. As a university within a city, its students also have easy access to the capital's many amenities.

Student accommodation
There are three halls of residence that offer full-time accommodation – these are very popular with first year students. The cost starts around $180 per week.

Flatting is also very popular. Shared flats can cost anywhere from $90 per week not including living expenses. Private board is available, and the cost usually includes two meals per day with three at the weekend – from around $165 per week. Further information can be obtained from the International Students office, Victoria University, PO Box 600, Wellington. Tel: 64-4-471 5350.

Massey University, Palmerston North

Founded in 1927, Massey Agricultural College was named after a former Prime Minister of New Zealand, William Ferguson Massey. The College offered degree programmes leading to Bachelor and Master of Agricultural Science and students could also enrol in a variety of shorter courses in farm management and technology. Courses in horticulture were introduced after the war.

Massey College became a University in early 1964. Massey is the leading provider of extramural or 'university correspondence' courses in the southern hemisphere.

Massey is now New Zealand's second largest tertiary institution. It occupies a 40 hectare campus. The University farms 5,250 hectares of land of which 900 hectares surround the campus. This area has a full range of agricultural enterprises including dairy farms, sheep and cattle farms, a cropping unit, orchard and a deer facility. As well as operating as commercial enterprises the farms are an extension of the lecture theatre, providing facilities for student demonstrations and research.

Student accommodation
The University has halls of residence with places for a limited number of students. In recent years demand has often exceeded supply so an application must be made. These are available from the University Liaison Officer or Residential Services Office. The closing date for applications is towards the end of October.

A single room costs roughly $160 per week and includes breakfast and an evening meal. Accommodation outside the campus can be found within the surrounding area of Palmerston North. For further information contact the Registrars Office, Massey University, Palmerston North, NZ. Website: *www.massey.ac.nz.*

STUDENT BUDGETING

If you have a typical student's income and costs, you will spend most of your money on accommodation and food. Use the budget form below to work out your budget. The sample budgets are based on Victoria University, and so could change with other universities.

An approximation of living costs
Halls of residence

$	185.00	Per week for a single room
$	150.00	Per week for a shared room
$	200.00	Placement fee and Activities fee
$	30.00	Per semester for communal laundry facilities
$	110.50	Per semester for uncovered off-street parking
$	15.00	Per semester for a lockable bike shed

Flatting

$	78.00	Per week, per room sharing with 4–6 people
$	156.00	Placement fee
$	10.00	Per week for telephone

$ 15.00	Per week for electricity
$ 25.00	Per week for transport

University costs

$ 167.00	Student services fee
$ 15,000.00	Tuition (approx.)
$ 50.00	Textbooks per semester
$ 310.00	Insurance travel, health, personal, per semester

Now fill in the form which follows to see what your budget will be.

How to prepare your budget

1. Work out your income for the academic year:

	INCOME
Savings from vacation work	$
Income tax refund	$
Other income: interest, dividends, trust loans	$
Gifts, allowances from parents/relatives	$
Student allowances	$
A or B bursary award	$
Other scholarship or awards	$
Income part-time jobs	$
Total income for academic year	$ ___

2. Work out your likely expenses for the academic year:

Tuition fees	$
Students' Association fee	$
Student services levy	$
Textbooks, stationery	$
Hall of residence deposit	$
Hall heating and linen charge	$
Hall residents fee	$
Bond for flat and agent's fee	$
Deposit: gas, electricity, phone	$
Total fixed expenses	$ ___

Sample budget 'A'

This sample given below is based on minimum costs. The headings are the usual area of student expenses. There is a possibility that these costs will change from year to year.

This budget assumes that a student has a shared room in the halls of residence for the 32 weeks of the academic year, not including the May and August vacations or mid-year break.

Weekly expenses	*per week $*	*32 weeks $*
Hall board	185.00	5,920.00
Snacks	20.00	640.00
Entertainment, postage *etc*	30.00	960.00
Subtotal	235.00	7,520.00

Fixed expenses	
Students services fee	167.00
Tuition fee (approx.)	15,000.00
Building levy	56.00
Resources fee	210.00
Textbooks, stationery *etc*	400.00
Hall deposit	200.00
Subtotal	16,033.00

Periodic payments (not all essential)	
Insurance	310.00
Holidays	500.00
Sports, recreation, hobbies	170.00
Subscriptions for clubs *etc*	40.00
Clothes, footwear *etc*	500.00
Health: dentist, doctor	300.00
Subtotal	1,820.00

Approximate total expenditure	25,373.00

Sample budget 'B'

This sample budget is based on minimum costs, assuming that a student shares a flat with at least two others for an average of 37 weeks, and that the flat is given up or sub-let over the summer vacation.

Weekly expenses	Per week $	37 weeks $
Rent	120.00	4,440.00
Food (communal)	60.00	2,220.00
Lunches, snacks *etc*	35.00	1,295.00
Telephone rental (share of)	10.00	370.00
Electricity (share of)	15.00	555.00
Local travel (academic year only)	25.00	925.00
Entertainment, postage, toiletries	30.00	1110.00
Subtotal	295.00	10,915.00
Fixed expenses (see example 'A')		16,033.00
Periodic payments (see example 'A')		1,820.00
Approximate total expenditure		28,768.00

QUESTIONS AND ANSWERS

Is there help for children with reading problems?

Yes, there are specialist teachers attached to schools throughout New Zealand who provide long-term assistance for children with serious reading problems.

What courses does the Correspondence School offer?

The Correspondence School, or The Open Polytechnic of New Zealand (TOPNZ), offers over 800 courses from certificate to degree level. Subjects range from the new Bachelor of Business degree, real estate, hairdressing and agriculture, to plumbing and airline pilot's licences. There are over 350 tutors and 120 support staff, educating more than 25,000 students every year.

5

Housing and Living

BUYING A HOUSE

Whilst writing this book I and my family rented a house in a Wellington suburb. It was high on a hilltop with delightful views of the surrounding hills and with a glimpse of Wellington Harbour. The views were great and so we thought was the house, for which we paid $220 per week. It had a very generous sized lounge, with big windows facing the Harbour. It was 'U' shaped with a dining/kitchen facing the hills (at the back of the house).

The large attractive bathroom had all-day sun, with a separate toilet. The back bedroom which was only a single also saw the sun for most of the day, and overlooked the hills at the back. The middle (slightly larger) bedroom only saw the sun in the early morning and the large main bedroom had a small window that only caught the early morning sun, with a large window overlooking the Harbour which was totally sunless. The warmest place in this house was undoubtedly the bathroom, and on cold days I could often be found sitting in there warming myself! My eldest daughter had even tried it out for saxophone practice!

As a result of this experience, I would always check now to see how the sun affected a property.

The windows in this house were very badly warped and seldom fitted properly. This meant that when the wind blew – and that was fairly often – the curtains would billow without the windows being opened!

Also, the house wasn't insulated. Consequently the rooms that saw the sun only briefly were cold and damp-smelling, especially in the winter, with mildew on the walls.

Never mind the view!
During the two years I sold real estate (houses only) I viewed literally hundreds of houses, and here are a few very important tips to bear in mind when you are buying:

- Is the house insulated?

- Does it face the sun – never mind the view!

- Does it have heating? (Very important if you are buying in the cooler areas, *ie* from Auckland south.)

- If you are buying in Wellington, especially, ensure that it isn't in the path of the prevailing wind, never mind the view!

- Look for damp and mouldy patches inside and outside.

- Make sure that building permits have been obtained where alterations or additions have been made.

- A property which lies below the level of the road is not always desirable.

- Make sure that the house isn't sheltered from the sun by the surrounding hills – a great possibility in Wellington.

- Check that all windows open and close properly.

- Check the house foundations, especially older houses built on piles. (Engage a builder or surveyor to check this out for you.)

- If it has a weatherboard or wooden exterior, check to see that there are no rotten patches – a poke with a pencil will show weaknesses. (Again, it would be advisable to get an expert to check this out.)

- Make sure that the house is *above* ground level. A house that is level with the footpaths will probably let rain in under floors.

- Wellington has the most amazing selection of houses dotted around the numerous hills. Some of them appear to be hanging from sky hooks! Make sure they are not! A Building Inspector from the City Council will check out the foundations and retaining walls for you.

Rainy days are best!
Whilst selling real estate I acquired a client, a dear old lady, who had been looking for the 'right' place for some time, but was in no hurry. I rang her one day with news of a very nice property. The day was fine and sunny, a real estate agent's dream, and I conveyed the good news.

To my disappointment she said the day wasn't 'right'. I enquired why, and she said she would only go looking on rainy days! I was

PROPERTY MARKET

NORTHERN

Whangarei $160,000: Huge home, multi-storey, mod. 3-bed, lounge, dining, conservatory, ensuite Handy amenities.

Auckland-Avondale $295,000: Luxury home, 4-bed, double garage, internal access, open plan living.

Ak-Mt Albert $390,000: Wonderful family home on large section. 3-4 beds, large living, great location.

Ak-City $300,000: Fully furnished 1-bed and carpark, hotel managed, north-west corner. Offers over.

Ak-Parnell $475,000: Multi-level contemporary style property, quiet bushy location. 4-beds, office, 2-baths.

Ak-Remuera $610,000: Northern slopes, flat section, prime, private and peaceful location. 3-beds + sunroom, spacious living.

Tauranga $395,000: Waterfront home. 3-bed, study, ensuite, pathway to beach.

Mt Maunganui $299,000: Quality home, 4-bed, sep. lounge, ensuite, many extras here.

Rotorua $230,000: 4-bed, sep. lounge, dining, study, inground thermal pool.

Hamilton $212,000: Split level 4-bed, sep. lounge, dining/kitchen, inground pool.

CENTRAL

Hastings $295,000: 3-bed, sep. lounge, conservatory, executive home with great views. Self contained flat.

Napier $320,000: Country living almost in town. Some 4.72 hectares of land with a private, 4-bed Lockwood home. Swimming pool.

New Plymouth $180,000: Single level villa, circa around 1918, partially restored, indoor/outdoor flow. 3-4 beds, close amenities.

Wanganui $235,000: College estate, multi-storey, a grand home offering plenty. 3-beds, sep. lounge, sep. dining, office, 2 sep. toilets.

Palmerston North $235,000: Split level timber home, 3-beds, sep. lounge, large section, deck fenced.

Lower Hutt $275,000: Modern split level home, 3-beds, lounge/dining, lovely setting amongst quality residences. Master ensuite, harbour views.

Wellington-Hataitai $380,000: Multi-storey contemporary house, 4-beds, sep. lounge, study, conservatory, outstanding family home.

Wgtn-Khandallah $725,000: Multi-storey, both formal and informal living, indoor/outdoor entertaining, family room, big games room, 5-beds.

SOUTH

Nelson $348,000: 3-bed, sep. lounge, sep. dining, study, ensuite, close city centre with great views.

Blenheim $269,000: Fantastic view, great street appeal, lots of features, 2-beds, rumpus/family, sep. lounge & dining.

Christchurch-Avonhead $319,000: Immaculate sun catcher, two storey house with many extras. Beside stream. 4-beds, 2 lounges.

Chch-Fendalton $790,000: Gracious family home with original interior detailing. 4 living areas, stream boundary. 5-beds, ensuite.

Chch-Halswell $207,000: 3-bed, bungalow, tastefully done throughout, sunny living, nice kitchen and bathroom.

Timaru $285,000: Near new executive home, absolute impeccable presentation, 3-4 beds (ensuite), courtyard.

Queenstown $995,000: A lovely home in Tuscany style with five bedrooms and 2 bathrooms, triple garage. Two acres.

Queenstown $395,000: 3-bed home nestled amongst a mature cottage style garden, large outdoor living with unsurpassed lake views.

Dunedin-Waverley $175,000: Modern 4-bed, family home situated on beautifully landscaped section. All day sun.

Dunedin-Mornington $89,500: Newly renovated home, 2-beds, modern kitchen, spacious dining and living.

Invercargill $399,000: Prime city real estate. One of the landmarks, beautiful brick character mansion with ballroom, Would be over $1 million anywhere else. 6-beds, 5 sep. toilets.

Fig. 20. Houses for sale – typical examples.

surprised at this response, and asked why. She told me that lots of houses looked good on warm sunny days, but it took a special place to look good on a grey wet day! I rang her the next 'bad' day, and along she came dressed in her gum boots and wet weather gear!

Who stole the third bedroom?

There have been many cases of people buying a house only to put it straight back on the market again. This may sound strange, but when people don't take the time to visit a property more than once, before buying, errors of judgment can occur.

One couple were in such a hurry to buy, the husband being a very busy man, that they only saw the property once and then bought it. Were their faces red when they couldn't find the all important third bedroom, as it was only a two-bedroomed house!

Single and double storey

Houses can be single or double storey. Double storey houses quite often have garages on the ground floor, with a laundry, rumpus room (games room), possibly a workshop and maybe one bedroom. All the living and sleeping areas are on the first floor.

- If the advertisement just says 'house for sale' with no mention of two floors, then you can expect this to be a bungalow, *ie* with everything on one floor.

- Units are semi detached, or can be found in blocks of four or more, single or double storey, on small sections.

- Townhouses can be one or two storey, free standing or attached by a garage on a small section. Some real estate agents advertise townhouses as being 'joined' (semi detached). Townhouses are usually slightly more upmarket than units.

Villas

The older style homes, which are now referred to as 'villas', were built of wood, usually Kauri, which is now regarded as one of New Zealand's antique woods. They would typically have a corrugated iron roof which was painted.

They would also quite often have lovely ornate turn-of-the-century verandahs, reminiscent of Scarlett O'Hara, where the early settler families would sit and relax out of the heat of the day.

These homes today are keenly sought after and highly regarded as they look wonderful when renovated. They have the advantage of

FOURTH EDITION MAY 1991

AGREEMENT FOR SALE AND PURCHASE OF REAL ESTATE

This form is approved by the Real Estate Institute of New Zealand and by the New Zealand Law Society.

DATE:

VENDOR:

PURCHASER:

Address of property:

Legal description: *Estate:* **FREEHOLD (unless otherwise described)**

Area   *Lot:*   *DP:*   *CT:*

Purchase Price: $ *(including chattels at $*

Delete one of these: **Plus GST** (if any).   OR   **Inclusive of GST** (if any).

If neither is deleted the purchase price includes GST (if any).

Deposit: $

Balance of purchase price to be paid or satisfied as follows:

LSP date: **GST date:**

Possession date: **Interest rate for late settlement**   **% p.a.**

Special conditions: *(if any)*   **SEE OVERLEAF**

Fig. 21. Agreement for sale and purchase of real estate.

106

Financial conditions

LAST DAY FOR ARRANGING FINANCE:

Lender: Amount required: $

Lender: Amount required: $

All mortgages on the customary terms and conditions of the lender(s).

Details of tenancies: *(if any)* **Name of tenant:**

Rent: **Term:**   **Right of renewal:**

CHATTELS The following chattels if now situated on the property, are included in the sale *(strike out or add as applicable)*:

STOVE   TV AERIALS   FIXED FLOOR COVERINGS   BLINDS   CURTAINS   DRAPES   LIGHT FITTINGS

Sale by (name of real estate agent):

It is agreed that the vendor sells and the purchaser purchases the above described property, and the chattels included in the sale, on the terms set out above, on the general conditions attached and any special conditions hereinafter appearing.

WARNINGS *(These warnings do not form part of this contract)*

1 This is a binding contract. If either party has any doubts professional advice should be sought **before signing.**

2. Before signing this contract the purchaser should make sure that the status of the property under the Town and Country Planning Act 1977 is satisfactory for the purchaser's intended use of it.

Signature of vendor(s)   **Signature of purchaser(s)**

....

....

large spacious rooms with high ceilings, and make excellent family homes. They usually have separate laundries, a definite advantage, especially if you have lived in a house with the clothes dryer in the kitchen: when the day is wet and cold, and all the doors are closed, the rest of the house ends up streaming in condensation.

There are many of these old villas in Wellington, and they have been painted in very interesting colour schemes, with modern drapes, and they look quite wonderful. It would be great fun to renovate an old villa.

The quarter acre paradise

New Zealand has always been referred to as 'the quarter acre paradise'. This refers to the size of the sections of land once normal throughout New Zealand.

Some houses can still be found on the quarter acre sized section, mainly in less popular areas. However, in the popular areas people have been able to cut their sections in half, just retaining enough land around the original house, and perhaps using the back half of their land to sell to someone who could then build a small unit or townhouse type of property. Of course if the access around the sides of the original house is not wide enough, then this cannot be done, as driveways have to be considered when this type of sub-division is undertaken.

It got to a stage when everyone was rushing to sell off part of their land, and so the sections got smaller and smaller. The Government finally stepped in to ensure that homes still had an adequate amount of land around them and stipulated that sections had to be a minimum of 690 square metres.

There is another special way of buying a home in New Zealand, and that is to choose your piece of land, and then find a house, usually an older type villa, that has been moved from its land, and stored in a builder's yard. It is then advertised for sale, the cost of removal to your land being included in the price.

It is not unusual to see a whole house – or a house cut in half with one half on one transporter and the other on another transporter – moving slowly along the road, usually at night or on quiet days, to its new site. Houses have even been shipped out by barge to someone who has chosen to live on one of the islands around this coast.

It is quite a sight to watch someone else's choice of wallpaper and curtains on full view going down the road, maybe half the kitchen with all its cupboard doors opening and banging shut, being driven down the main street of some small town.

Choosing building materials

The older style homes are quite often built of weatherboards with corrugated iron roofs. Modern houses are now being built of cheaper materials, *ie* sheets of composition materials which are then sprayed with fibre cement, and then painted, to give a Mediterranean look. Brick is used, but it is much more expensive; in lots of houses you will find perhaps one feature wall, usually the front door area, in brick. To build with brick would cost about $130 per square metre against $110 per square metre for the sprayed finish. Wood, too, is now becoming too expensive to build with, and so this too is often used for a feature wall.

The insides of the houses comprise a 'shell' of wooden framework with sheets of plasterboard attached. Roofing materials can vary, with corrugated iron being the cheapest, then followed by Decramastic (textured steel tiles) and concrete tiles with a baked enamel finish.

Real estate jargon

Section	Plot or piece of land
Gge	Garage
Corr	Corrugated
T/House	Town house
Pte	Private
Dble	Double
Brm	Bedroom
Lge	Large
Do up special	Handyman special for renovation
X-leasable	Section large enough to cut in half and sell half
Cnd	Condition
Mort	Mortgage
Redec	Redecorated
Qual	Quality
Ens	Ensuite
Incl	Include
Psn	Position
Spa	Jacuzzi
B and T	Brick building with tile roof
Sleepout	An outside room
Villa	Older style wooden house
Rumpus room	Play room
G V	Government valuation of the property
Crosslease	A half a section

Sep. Title	A cross-leased section with its own title
Back Section	A property built on a section behind other homes (no road frontage)
Bach & Crib	A holiday style cottage
Whiteware	Washing machine, dishwasher, fridge, cooker
Right of Way	A driveway which runs through other sections to give access to a back section
Woodburner	A wood burning fire which sometimes provides hot water
TLC	Tender loving care

HOUSING AND FURNISHING COSTS

Obviously there are always exceptions to the rules, and with house prices there aren't even any rules. Where you want to live, and how popular an area is, sets the prices for houses. In Auckland, for instance, a three-bedroom house in South Auckland would cost a lot less than a three-bedroom house in Remuera. So the prices quoted here are only for average homes in the middle price range areas.

In Wellington the cost would be approximately $186,000. Prices in Auckland would be roughly around $235,000. In Taranaki the prices are less, with an average of $108,000. Manawatu around $107,000. In the South Island prices are usually less, and a house in Christchurch would be $140,000 and in Dunedin even less at $95,000. Obviously, if you are a cash buyer, then you are in an admirable position to barter, and you could end up with a really good buy. Real estate sales have slowed down over the last few years, and it is certainly a buyers' market.

If you write to a New Zealand newspaper and request a copy every now and then, you will be able to see at a glance how prices vary. See Chapter 3 for the addresses of newspapers, and the cost involved.

Furnishing your home

Furniture	*$*
Lounge suite – two chairs and settee	2,000–5,000
Dining table and six chairs	1,500–4,000
Queensize bed	800–3,000
Children's bunks	500
Single bed	400–2,000

Baby's cot	300
Three-drawer dressing table with mirror	900
Six-drawer chest of drawers	800–1,500

Household goods

Woolrest fleecy underblanket (queen)	310
Blankets 100% wool	119
Duvets – single	159
– queen	249
Sheets – single	50
– queen	70
– cotton single	45
– cotton queen	49
Towels – hand	3–39
– bath	10–45

Electrical goods

Mitsubishi television 21″	449
Mitsubishi television 25″	899
Philips television 14″	392
Philips stereo	399–800
Philips stereo with CD, double deck, 2-way speakers	400–800
Philips AM/FM radio cassette	199
Panasonic microwave	599
Fisher and Paykel Autowasher	1,049
Fisher and Paykel A39	449
Fisher and Paykel A55	549
Kelvinator fridge freezer	1,549
Fisher and Paykel dishwasher	1,299
Fisher and Paykel fan oven	1,149
Sunbeam kettle – fast boil	70
Sunbeam toaster	90
Sunbeam iron – steam/dry	60
Sunbeam food processor	279
Red Devil vacuum cleaner	179
Breville cake mixer	229
Remmington hairdryer	100
Wall mounted towel rail	80
Electric blanket – single	100
– queen	159
Goldair fan heater	50

Kitchen

Three piece stainless steel saucepan set	140
20-piece dinner set	120

Miscellaneous

Steelcraft Calais Stroller	430
Victa two-stroke motor mower	599

In New Zealand, as anywhere else, it pays to shop around. Prices vary according to quality and the above prices are in the economy range.

I haven't forgotten to include the cost of wardrobes. In New Zealand most homes have built-in wardrobes.

Don't bring the kitchen sink!

It will probably be very hard to decide what you should bring with you. I can remember finding more and more belongings that I felt I just couldn't live without! My poor husband had to keep collecting yet another crate, with the strict instructions that this had to be the last! We did our own packing, and as the carrier was collecting the cases at 7 am my husband stayed up all night nailing down all the lids and painting names and addresses on the sides. We travelled here by sea and we were allowed a certain amount of luggage to be stored in the holds free of charge, so we took advantage of that!

Is it really worth it? For example, that lumpy old bed with the dip in the middle, that has always hurt your back, and that old wardrobe left to you by Grandma. Upgrade your bed: it could cost you as little as $800, and as I have already said, most homes here have built-in wardrobes.

You will need to change all the plugs on your electrical appliances when you arrive here, so you might as well give them to someone back home.

New Zealand power phase is 230 volts, 50 cycles. To ensure that your electrical appliances are compatible, consult an electrician in your own country, to save you the cost of bringing appliances to New Zealand that cannot be used.

Mortgage finance

Borrowing money on mortgage is a principal means of financing the building or purchase of houses and commercial buildings, and the purchase of farms. The main sources of mortgage finance for houses are registered banks and other institutions, *ie* saving institutions, finance companies and merchant banks.

RENTING

Rental costs

There is plenty of property to rent in all newspapers. Prices vary according to areas, and style of house you want to rent. You can rent a fabulous 'mansion' style place with five bedrooms and five bathrooms, swimming pool and four-car garage if you have $1,500–$2,000 per week to spend. A medium-priced three-bed home for the average type family will cost approximately $350 per week in Auckland, $240 per week in Hamilton, $180 per week in New Plymouth, $220 per week in Palmerston North, $340 per week in Wellington, $200 per week in Christchurch and $120 per week in Dunedin.

If you are looking for a shared situation, you will pay around $80 to $120 per week, without costs, for a single room.

Bonds and fees

When you rent you will have to pay two weeks' bond, which is held by the Housing Corporation and returned to you when you leave the property, provided that it is left in the same condition in which you took it. If you find a property through the services of a real estate agent, then you will also have that fee to pay. It is usually one week's rent, *ie* if you are paying $200 per week rent, then you will pay $200 to the real estate agent.

REAL ESTATE AGENTS

Here are the names and addresses of the three largest real estate organisations in New Zealand.

Century 21

PB 1596, Palmerston North 5330. Tel: 64-6-356 4829.
PO Box 2506, Tauranga. Tel: 64-7-578 7000.
PO Box 21 087, Christchurch. Tel: 64-3-379 2121.
PO Box 68, Papakura, Auckland. Tel: 64-9-298 4209.
PO Box 35, Hamilton. Tel: 64-7-855 9013.
PO Box 2346, Rotorua. Tel: 64-7-347 7699.
PO Box 1332, Takapuna, Auckland. Tel: 64-9-486 6079.
PO Box 763, Invercargill. Tel: 64-3-218 6203.

Challenge Realty

PB 30 125, Lower Hutt. Tel: 64-4-569 9139.
PO Box 18, Greymouth. Tel: 64-3-768 4035.

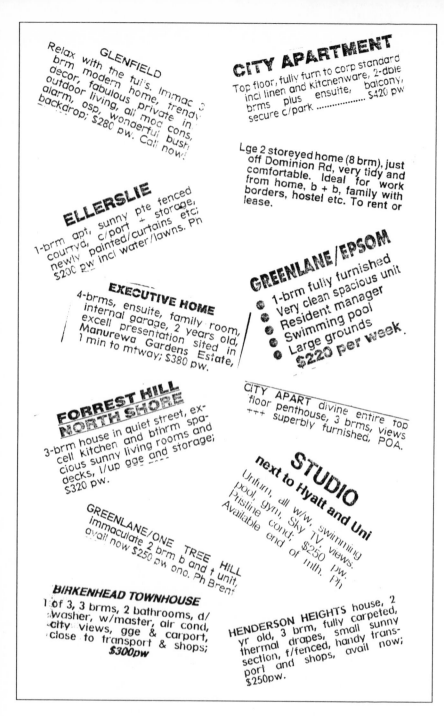

GLENFIELD
Relax with the tui's. Immac 3 brm modern home, trendy decor, fabulous private in outdoor living, all mod cons, alarm, osp, wonderful bush backdrop; $280 pw. Call now!

CITY APARTMENT
Top floor, fully furn to corp standard incl linen and kitchenware, 2-dble brms plus ensuite, balcony, secure c/park .... $420 pw

Lge 2 storeyed home (8 brm), just off Dominion Rd, very tidy and comfortable. Ideal for work from home, b + b, family with borders, hostel etc. To rent or lease.

ELLERSLIE
1-brm apt, sunny pte fenced courtyd, c/port + storage, newly painted/curtains etc; $200 pw incl water/lawns. Ph

GREENLANE/EPSOM
● 1-brm fully furnished
● Very clean spacious unit
● Resident manager
● Swimming pool
● Large grounds
$220 per week

EXECUTIVE HOME
4-brms, ensuite, family room, internal garage, 2 years old, excell presentation sited in Manurewa Gardens Estate, 1 min to mtway; $380 pw.

FORREST HILL NORTH SHORE
3-brm house in quiet street, excell kitchen and bthrm spacious sunny living rooms and decks, l/up gge and storage; $320 pw.

CITY APART divine entire top floor penthouse, 3 brms, views +++ superbly furnished, POA.

STUDIO
next to Hyatt and Uni
Unfurn, all w/w, swimming pool, gym, Sky TV, views; Pristine cond; $250 pw. Available end of mth. Ph

GREENLANE/ONE TREE HILL immaculate 2 brm b and t unit, avail now $250 pw ono. Ph Brent

BIRKENHEAD TOWNHOUSE
1 of 3, 3 brms, 2 bathrooms, d/washer, w/master, air cond, city views, gge & carport, close to transport & shops; **$300pw**

HENDERSON HEIGHTS house, 2 yr old, 3 brm, fully carpeted, thermal drapes, small sunny section, f/fenced, handy transport and shops, avail now; $250pw.

Fig. 22. Properties to rent – typical examples.

Tenancy Agreement

Landlord's name:

Occupation:

Address (being an address for service, not a PO Box number):

Phone number:

Tenant's name:

Occupation:

Address (being an address for service):

Phone number:

Address of rented premises:

Furniture etc, provided by landlord (if any):

The Landlord and the Tenant agree that:

1. This tenancy shall commence on   /   /19
2. The rent shall be $ per week/fortnight.
3. The rent shall be paid weekly/fortnightly in advance.
4. The rent shall be placed at the following place or into the following bank account number:
5. The tenant shall pay a bond of $
6. The tenant shall not assign (transfer) or sublet tenancy without first gaining the landlord's written permission.
7. The tenant shall pay the solicitor's fee (if any) or the real estate agent's fee (if any) relating to the grant of this tenancy.
8. This tenancy is subject to the Residential Tenancies Act 1986.
9. Other conditions of this tenancy:

Dated: /   /19   (Landlord) ....

Signed: (Tenant) ....

Form supplied by

TEN·NCY
services

A division of the Ministry of Housing

T04(8/92)

Fig. 23. A tenancy agreement.

PO Box 298, Wanaka 9192. Tel: 64-3-443 8511.
PO Box 21-158, Henderson, Auckland. Tel: 64-9-837 0726.
PB 1655, Dunedin. Tel: 64-3-477 4303.

Harcourts Real Estate
PB 5267, Dunedin. Tel: 64-3-477 5334.
PO Box 885, Tauranga 3015. Tel: 64-7-576 8770.
PO Box 33-114, Barrington, Christchurch. Tel: 64-3-332 1525.
PO Box 33-198, Takapuna, Auckland. Tel: 64-9-480 7426.
PO Box 10-777, Wellington. Tel: 64-4-476 8752.
PO Box 8054, Riccarton, Christchurch. Tel: 64-3-348 8784.
PO Box 396, Taupo 2730. Tel: 64-7-378 4170.
PO Box 610, New Plymouth 9999. Tel: 64-6-758 5206.

THE WEEKLY SHOPPING BASKET

Item	Price	Item	Price
500g butter	$1.45	1kg tomatoes	$7.95
1kg cheese	$4.99	lettuce	$2.25
500g margarine	$1.80	cauliflower	$0.99
750g weetabix	$1.89	1.5kg carrots	$0.79
1 litre milk	$1.45	1.5kg onions	$0.79
275g jar of jam	$1.79	1kg apples	$0.99
12 medium eggs	$1.79	200g instant coffee	$6.99
2 litre icecream	$2.79	100 tea bags	$2.89
1kg frozen peas	$1.00	8 toilet rolls	$1.79
500g frozen sweet corn	$1.10	small bottle bleach	$2.00
5 kg flour	$3.89	softly wool wash	$4.30
3 kg raw sugar	$2.49	1kg washing powder	$3.45
400g tin cat food	$1.54	large loaf of bread	$2.30
1kg beef top side	$7.89	pkt chocolate chip biscuits	$2.39
1kg rumpsteak	$8.77	1kg bacon	$10.95
1kg sausages	$2.49	bottle of white wine	$7.99
per kg no. 14 size chicken	$4.49	bottle of gin 1125ml	$26.95
per kg lamb roast	$6.99	bottle of vodka 1125ml	$28.95
per kg lamb chops	$5.79		
per kg pork shoulder roast	$6.45	*fish prices*	
2kg mince beef	$10.00	shrimps (kg)	$19.95
bottle of red wine	$13.95	salmon (kg)	$19.95
300g milo	$1.45	oysters (doz)	$10.95
1kg banana	$1.39		

All prices fluctuate, these are only approximates.

QUESTIONS AND ANSWERS

Is the quality of New Zealand clothing good?

Yes, there is a very high standard, and a lot of emphasis on pure wool and cotton.

Are all the houses sold through estate agents?

No, there is some property on the market without the services of a real estate agent. Quite a lot of people try to sell their property themselves when first they decide, in order to avoid the real estate agent's fee.

6

Health and Welfare

HOW HEALTH CARE IS ORGANISED

The New Zealand health system is made up of public, private and voluntary sectors which interact to provide and fund health care.

Department of Health

The Department is the principal adviser to the Minister of Health on health issues. It administers relevant legislation, funds programmes and ensures the provision of essential services. It collects and disseminates information, liaises and consults on health matters, monitors and reviews health programmes and is responsible for ensuring that its work is underpinned by a focus on the Government's desired health outcomes.

Regional Health Authorities

In July 1993 four Regional Health Authorities were established as independent Crown Agencies with their own Board of Directors.

The primary objective of Regional Health Authorities is to ensure that the population in their regions receives optimum value from the health and disability support services funding, entrusted to the Regional Health Authorities within the parameters of Government policy. The RHAs purchase health procedures by way of tendering for services and contracting with health care providers, *ie* hospitals (CHEs), rest homes, *etc.*

Other care providers

Health care provided by general practitioners is also partially funded from the public purse, as are referrals to specialists and laboratory diagnostic services. Dental care is provided free to dependent children under 18 years of age. Eighty per cent of the cost of pharmaceuticals is met through public funding. A number of private hospital services are subsidised, and a range of private and voluntary organisations receive funding for services they are contracted to provide.

Accident compensation levies cover 4.2% of health care costs for services provided in the public and private sectors.

The private sector provides a wide range of health care options. Forty-five per cent of the population has private health insurance, meeting 3.5% of the total cost of health care.

An active voluntary sector incorporates a wide range of organisations which provide care, support, health education and research. Health care is also provided informally by families and relatives, and this is recognised through the growing provision of home support services in the public and voluntary sectors.

Health expenditure

General taxation funds an estimated 77% of the total costs of health care. This funding is primarily disbursed through the Department of Health, which distributes funds to area health boards, and a wide range of health professionals and organisations providing services to the public. It also includes funding for health related expenditure through other government departments such as Social Welfare, Defence and Police. Accident compensation levies cover 4.2% of health care costs.

Over recent years governments have introduced a number of measures to curb health spending, while maintaining services. Area health board funding, which makes up nearly 70% of the Department of Health's budget allocation, has come in for particular attention.

A population-based method is used to determine funding for the boards. It takes into account the age and gender of the population in each region, by adjusting for the expected resource use of each age/gender group, derived from national levels. Special health needs are also considered, through calculations based on socio-economic factors.

In 1992 the Government expanded the ability of the boards to charge each other for cross-boundary service provision. From February 1992, the boards began receiving revenue from inpatient and outpatient user charges.

Service statements have been developed by the Department of Health, in consultation with health service providers. These are designed to provide guidance to the area health boards on the content and structure of services provided by each board. The statements provide a national perspective on the key elements comprising a service, as well as the policy and legislative parameters for each service. Each board will design and provide the services in accordance with its own strategic and financial planning processes. These may reflect their assessment of local needs and resource priorities.

NEW ZEALAND'S HEALTH & WELFARE SCHEME

The Department of Social Welfare, which reports to the Minister in charge of the department, exists to assist Government to achieve its goals in meeting the welfare needs of New Zealanders.

These social security goals fall broadly into three groups:

1. To ensure that all the people of New Zealand receive an adequate income.

2. To provide and deliver welfare services and support to the community.

3. To allocate and deliver resources and support to community groups and organisations and enhance their ability to deliver Social Services.

The **New Zealand Income Support Service** provides for:

- National Superannuation
- Unemployment Benefit
- Domestic Purposes Benefit
- Invalids Benefit
- Sickness Benefit
- Widows Benefit.

Reciprocity Agreements
United Kingdom

The **Social Security (Reciprocity with United Kingdom) Act 1983** provides for reciprocity in a comprehensive range of benefits. The general principle of the convention is that people migrating from one country to another will be taken into the social security scheme of the receiving country, and paid benefits under the laws and conditions applicable to other residents of that country (not the home country).

In essence, if you have lived for the last ten years in the country with the reciprocal agreement, you will be automatically entitled to receive **income assistance**. If you do not live in a country with a reciprocal agreement you will need to have lived in New Zealand for ten years before you qualify.

Reciprocal agreements are also in place for citizens of Australia and the Netherlands (in some categories only).

For further information call:

Income Support Service
International Affairs Office
Free phone: 64-0800 552 002.

Superannuation

The benefit rates are:

	Net NZ$
• single person living alone	225.55 pw
• single person sharing	208.20 pw
• married couple	347.00 pw

In 1987 the Labour Government decided, on the advice of the Minister of Finance Roger Douglas, to discontinue tax incentives for personal insurance and superannuation savings. Prior to this, person was allowed a tax rebate of $1,400 on personal super-annuation, and $1,200 on subsidised superannuation. The Government chose not to replace this with another scheme, and many people saw this as a disincentive to save.

The New Zealand Government is facing the same problem as many other countries, *ie* the increasing population of elderly people, which in turn places a big burden on the working population. The question now being asked is whether the New Zealand Government can continue to make superannuation payments indefinitely.

It is very obvious when you take the National Superannuation payment, and consider the cost of living (see chapter on Housing and Living Costs), that some extra savings must be made in order to able to retire with some dignity. There are many superannuation and insurance companies operating in New Zealand, and it certainly pays to shop around for the best deals.

Given below are some of the better known financial consultants and superannuation schemes:

Financial consultants
Money Concepts, 109 Molesworth Street, Thorndon, Wellington 6001. Tel: 64-4-473 0876. Fax: 64-4-473 0859.
Money Concepts, 169 Princess Street, Dunedin 9001. Tel: 64-3-477 5660.

Alexander & Alexander Ltd, PO Box 2845, Wellington 6015. Tel: 64-4-472 1699.

Alexander & Alexander Ltd, PO Box 2058, Christchurch 8015. Tel: 64-3-379 1420.

Superannuation schemes
AMP, PO Box 55, Auckland 1015. Tel: 64-9-377 4630.
AMP, PO Box 1499, Wellington 6015. Tel: 64-4-384 6369.
Tower Retirement Investment Ltd, PO Box 1086, Christchurch 8015. Tel: 64-3-365 4065.
Tower Retirement Investment Ltd, PO Box 742, Nelson 7016. Tel: 64-3-548 7025.

Unemployment benefit

The reciprocal agreement applies for citizens of the United Kingdom and Australia, which means that should the situation arise you would receive unemployment benefit. Citizens of other countries need to have lived in New Zealand for 12 months before they would become eligible.

For further information contact Work and Income New Zealand, PO Box 12-136, Wellington. Tel: 64-4-916 3300. Fax: 64-4-918 9779. Website: *www.winz.govt.nz*.

Domestic purposes benefit

The domestic purposes benefit is paid to:

- a parent caring for children without the support of a partner
- a person caring for someone at home who would otherwise be hospitalised
- an older woman alone – only in some cases.

The amount the beneficiary receives depends on:

- age
- whether they are married or have a partner
- number of children living with the recipient
- how much income they earn.

For further information contact Work and Income New Zealand, PO Box 12-136, Wellington. Tel: 64-4-916 3300. Fax: 64-4-918 9779. Website: *www.winz.govt.nz*.

Sickness benefit
This is for people who can't work and have had a drop in their earnings either because they are temporarily sick or injured, or because they are pregnant. The reciprocal agreement applies in this section also for Britain and Australia.

For further information contact Work and Income New Zealand, PO Box 12-136, Wellington. Tel: 64-4-916 3300. Fax: 64-4-918 9779. Website: *www.winz.govt.nz*.

Widows and bereaved families benefit
The widows benefit is paid to a woman whose husband or partner has died. The benefit helps those who have children to support or who have spent a number of years married or raising children – if the recipient does not have children, in order to qualify they must be over 50 years old. If the recipient has remarried then they are no longer entitled to receive this benefit.

For further information contact Work and Income New Zealand, PO Box 12-136, Wellington. Tel: 64-4-916 3300. Fax: 64-4-918 9779. Website: *www.winz.govt.nz*.

HEALTH SERVICE CHARGES FOR THE PATIENT
Visiting the doctor
The cost of a visit to a doctor in New Zealand varies depending on the doctor and possibly the area where you live. If you are on a low income and qualify for a **community services card**, you will pay a subsidised rate. If you do not, the approximate costs are as follows:

- senior citizen $30.00
- adult $60.00
- child under 5   free
- child 5–18 $30.00

If you just require a repeat prescription, then the charge (without seeing the doctor) will be $6. On top of this you will have to pay the cost of the drugs prescribed; each pharmacy has its own charges, depending on the drugs needed.

Visiting the dentist
There is no free dental treatment in New Zealand, and the cost of keeping your pearly smile can be horrendous. The figures shown are

approximate examples, as treatments can vary, and so can the dental costs. It certainly pays to check around first before making an appointment.

Procedure	Typical fee
Examination, X-ray and polish	$180.00
Normal filling	$200.00
Root filling	$1,500.00

Some private health schemes do cover dental treatment, so it would pay to check around before taking out cover if this would be a priority for you.

For further information contact the Dental Council of New Zealand, PO Box 10-448 Wellington, New Zealand. Tel: 64-4-499 4820. Fax: 64-4-499 1668.

Your state of health

Public health care in New Zealand is undergoing several changes, timed it seems with Government mood swings. It was decided in 1991 that hospitals should be run as businesses (that means paying tax). Several smaller community hospitals were closed down.

Waiting lists exist for many operations, and for some life-threatening situations, families have had to raise many thousands of dollars to send the patient overseas for treatment.

The benefits of private health schemes are quite obvious in such a situation. You then can have the special care you need without having to mortgage your home to get medical treatment. The schemes also pay a percentage of your visits to your doctor.

Medical insurance companies
These are a few medical insurance companies:

Medic Aid, 46 Smithfield Road, Wanganui 5001. Tel: 64-6-347 1895.
Southern Cross, PB 99-934, Newmarket, Auckland 1031. Tel: 64-9-356 0900.
Southern Cross, PO Box 27-145, Wellington. Tel: 64-4-384 4199. Fax: 64-4-385 0771.
Southern Cross, PO Box 1316, Dunedin 9015. Tel: 64-3-477 6365.
Southern Cross, PO Box 922. Ivercargill 9515. Tel: 64-3-218 3106.

Southern Cross, PO Box 1091, Hamilton 2015. Tel: 64-7-839 5108.
Aetna Health, PO Box 6772, Auckland. Tel: 64-9-302 8720.
AMP General Insurance, AMP Building, PO Box 1093, Wellington.
   Tel: 64-4-498 8000.

Typical costs of operations
Here are some typical costs for 'everyday' type surgery in a private
hospital:

Tonsils (child)	$ 1,590
(adult)	$ 1,795
Varicose veins	$ 2,170
Knee replacement	$ 12,520
Ingrown toenails	$ 710
Mastectomy	$ 1,930
Cardiac bypass	$ 21,445
Hip replacement	$ 11,585
Hysterectomy	$ 3,910

Hospital charges
Reciprocal agreement exists for citizens of England, Scotland, Wales
and Northern Ireland, as well as citizens of Australia to receive free
hospital treatment for emergency cases. This of course does not
cover a pre-known medical state, where you would have to pay for
treatment. Accidents are also covered in the A.I. Act under ACC
(the Accident Compensation Corporation).

   For citizens of other countries where a reciprocal agreement is
not in force, the costs can be large, *eg*:

	Excluding GST (12.5%)
Outpatient (flat rate)	$188–$300
Overnight stay (minimum)	$457–$3,704

On top of this will be the cost of treatment you may require.
Surgical costs can be from $3,700 per day for intensive and critical
care. X-rays, blood tests, CT scans, operating costs and pharmacy
costs are extra.

Eligibility for free treatment
• Those granted permanent residence or admitted as refugees by
   Immigration services.

- Cook, Nuie and Tokelau Islanders.

- Residents of Great Britain and Northern Ireland, including any premature births and complex maternity cases, but not including normal maternity care or those with a pre-existent condition.

- UK Royal Navy personnel.

- US Antarctic Expedition personnel.

- Those in possession of an extended work permit of two years or more. (The passport must be sighted for evidence of the permit.)

Not eligible for free treatment
- All other nationalities not mentioned previously, including citizens of the Commonwealth nations, Ireland, Japan, Fiji, Western Samoa, Tonga, New Caledonia, Tahiti, Kiribati and Vanuatu.

- NZ citizens or their dependants who have not themselves lived in NZ. Ordinarily, once a New Zealander, always a New Zealander, but those born to New Zealanders overseas must live in New Zealand to qualify.

- Those born in NZ or Australia, but now resident elsewhere (apart from NZ) or who have come here specifically for treatment.

- Diplomats.

- Fullbright scholars, except those from UK or Australia.

- Seamen from overseas ships. (Shipowner pays.)

- Those on temporary permits (*ie* student/work/visitor).

Work permits and visitor permits are normally issued for a maximum of one year only.

THE ACCIDENT COMPENSATION CORPORATION

We have a scheme here in New Zealand whereby everyone has $1.24

per $100 deducted from their earnings, and the employer also pays a proportion, *ie* from $1.18 to $5 per person per week depending on the type of work done; dangerous occupations will pay more.

In the event of an accident, the Accident Compensation Corporation pays for the treatment to the injured person; if that person is unable to work any more, then they are paid a percentage of their earnings up to a limit of around $86,000.

Some say that the scheme is good, but there have been many occasions when a person has been badly injured by, say, a car accident, and they are the innocent party. Under normal circumstances they could have sued that person, but Accident Compensation Corporation has taken away the right of a person to sue. So instead of a good lump sum payout, which might have paid for special equipment to help the injured person, the victim now has to be content with a weekly payment relative to the size of their earnings at the time of the accident subject to a maximum limit of approximately $86,000 per annum.

Example
In 1990, just to give you an illustration, I was driving along a secondary road, and whilst waiting to turn right was hit from behind. The resulting damage was whiplash resulting in a permanent weakness to the right shoulder/neck area. I claimed Accident Compensation. After being examined by a specialist – 12 months after the accident – I was awarded $12,000. Since then the terms of Accident Compensation have been changed, and people can no longer receive lump sum payments.

SUNSHINE CAMPS

The first health camp in New Zealand was organised by Dr Elizabeth Gunn in 1919. Dr Gunn was the school doctor for the Wanganui area; she believed that if delicate and undernourished children could be taught the basics of hygiene and nutrition and receive the benefit of rest and fresh air, many of their ailments would be cured. With the help of a local farmer, volunteer teachers and equipment hired from the army, Dr Gunn organised the camp at Turakina, near Wanganui. The camp was run along military lines with a bugle wake-up call in the morning, regimented eating and sleeping times, toothbrush drill, marching and flag saluting. After six weeks of camp-life the children flourished.

The success of Dr Gunn's health camps aroused public interest in the idea and by 1929 'sunshine camps', financed by private donations, were being run in several areas. 1929 also saw the first issue of health stamps by the Post Office with each stamp sold contributing one penny to the health camp fund. The first permanent camp was established at Otaki in 1932. By 1936 the movement was growing rapidly and a **National Health Camp Federation** was formed to oversee the burgeoning number of camps. In 1937 the King George V Memorial Fund raised 175,000 pounds sterling to establish permanent camps throughout the country.

The tradition of health camps that Dr Gunn established continues today. There are now seven permanent health camps at Whangarei, Pakuranga, Rotorua, Gisborne, Otaki, Christchurch and Roxburgh. Four to six week camps are held for children aged five to 12 years. The children are usually referred by teachers or doctors. Health camps today also help children with psychological or behavioural problems. As well as the games, schooling and health education that have always been part of the health camp regimen, children are now taught anger management, learning skills and life skills such as basic cooking and general personal hygiene. The Ministry of Education runs a special school in each camp where children with education problems can be given extra attention to develop positive attitudes towards schoolwork and learning. New Zealand Post continues to issue health stamps every spring, raising up to $100,000 a year for health camps and child health generally.

QUESTIONS AND ANSWERS

Is alternative medicine available in New Zealand?

Yes, very definitely. There is a very strong interest in acupuncture, aromatherapy, chiropractors and reflexology. There are also experts on herbal remedies.

Is dental treatment covered by the Health Department?

Only for children who are still at school. Everyone else must pay. Private health insurance can cover this.

Do I have to pay for medical treatment if I have an accident?

No. This type of treatment, whether in the hospital or from a doctor, is covered by Accident Compensation.

7

Living Under the Law

HOW THE LEGAL SYSTEM WORKS

New Zealand has inherited the British tradition of an independent judiciary, seen as a protection against unnecessary intrusion by the state into the lives of citizens. The Judicature Act 1908 and the Constitution Act 1986 contain a number of key provisions, designed to ensure judicial independence. Judges (including those who sit in the Court of Appeal) are appointed by the Governor-General, not the government. Neither Court of Appeal nor High Court judges may be removed from office except by the Sovereign or by the Governor General on grounds of misbehaviour or incapacity upon an address of the House of Representatives. District Court judges may be removed from office by the Governor-General, but only on the grounds of inability or misbehaviour.

The salaries of judges are determined by the Higher Salaries Commission under the Higher Salaries Commission Act 1977. Salaries may not be diminished during a judge's commission. No person may be appointed a judge unless he or she has held a practising certificate as a barrister or solicitor for at least seven years. The retirement age is 68, although former judges may be reappointed as acting judges for two years, or one year if the judge is 72 years of age when reappointed.

The court system

At the head of the hierarchy of courts of New Zealand is the Judicial Committee of the Privy Council. Below this is the Court of Appeal followed by the High Court, and the District Courts. All courts exercise both criminal and civil jurisdiction.

The Judicial Committee of the Privy Council
The Privy Council is the final appeal tribunal for New Zealand. Appeals to the Privy Council may be brought by leave of the court appealed from, or by special leave of the Privy Council itself. Leave

is granted as of right from any final judgement of the Court of Appeal, where the matter in dispute amounts to the value of $5,000 or more, or directly or indirectly involves some claim to property, or some civil right exceeding that value. The Privy Council has a discretionary power to grant special leave in criminal cases. Such leave is not often granted in criminal appeals from New Zealand.

The Court of Appeal
The highest appeal court in New Zealand, the Court of Appeal, has existed since 1846 and is constituted by the Judicature Amendment Act 1957.

Its primary function is to settle the law of New Zealand and to reconcile conflicting decisions of the other courts. It hears and determines ordinary appeals from the High Court. Certain other proceedings in the lower courts may, by order of the High Court, be removed to the Court of Appeal. The court does, however, also have some original jurisdiction.

The High Court
The High Court of New Zealand was first established (as the Supreme Court) in 1841. It has all the jurisdiction which may be necessary for a court to administer the laws of New Zealand.

The High Court exercises jurisdiction in cases of major crimes, Admiralty proceedings, the more important civil claims, appeals from lower courts and tribunals, and reviews of administrative actions. The High Court also has inherent jurisdiction to punish for contempt of court. It consists of the Chief Justice and 32 other judges, as prescribed by the Judicature Act 1908.

Specialist courts
These consist of the **Employment Court, the Family Courts, Youth Courts, Maori Land Court** and **Maori Appellate Court**.

Tribunals
Over 100 tribunals, authorities, boards, committees or related bodies exist to deal with other disputes, largely between individuals, on matters such as environmental planning, economic issues, scientific and technical matters, censorship, welfare and benefits, taxation, occupational licensing and discipline, activity licensing (*eg* shop trading hours) and company registration.

Jury service

Every person between the ages of 20 and 65 years (inclusive) is eligible for jury service, with some exceptions. Those who are not appropriate to serve on a jury because of their occupations are ineligible. A person may also be excused if jury service would cause serious inconvenience a or hardship, or if it is against a person's religious beliefs to serve on a jury. Also precluded are people with recent prison records and those who have been imprisoned for more than three years.

LEGAL AID IN NEW ZEALAND

The Legal Services Act 1991 brought together in one statute the civil and criminal legal aid schemes and aligned them as far as possible. It also gave statutory recognition to the **duty solicitor scheme** and to **community law centres**. The Act established new administrative structure – the **Legal Services Board** and **District Committees**. The Board is responsible for the legal aid budget. Its role is, however, wider. It can, or instance, investigate other ways of providing legal services to the public and set up pilot schemes.

Community Law Centres and Neighbourhood Law Offices

These offices and centres are set up to provide legal advice to people who cannot afford to go to a law firm. They are funded from a variety of sources and central government.

THE RISING CRIME RATE

When I came to this country in 1972, everyone was still talking about a 'big' murder case a few years earlier, when a man named Arthur Allen Thomas was convicted of murdering two people. He has since been acquitted.

New Zealand was in those days a very 'safe' country. People used to leave their house doors unlocked, and in fact some had never had a house key! People used to leave their cars unlocked when out shopping, there was never a problem with stealing.

Today, unfortunately, New Zealand has caught up with the rest of the world, and its crime rate is much increased. The sad thing is that the nation has become 'accustomed' to crime. New Zealanders today hardly bat an eyelid when hearing of people 'going berserk' and murdering several family members (this has happened about three times over the last two or three years). What has happened to this once 'safe' country?

According to *Statistics New Zealand*, in 1998 a total of 465,834 offences were recorded by the New Zealand Police, a decrease of 3.5% from the previous year. There were 2,012 robberies, 57,333 drug-related offences, 116 homicide offences, 741 recorded sexual offences and 45 murders.

Traffic offenders

New Zealand is a panel-beater's dream. I had never seen so many cars with body damage until I came to New Zealand. The trouble, of course, is with the drivers – not the cars! The attitude of drivers here has to be seen to be believed. They drive very aggressively, hoot behind you when you obey the speed limits, and drive up right behind you to make you hurry. This is probably one of the worst features of some drivers here. Nor will they let you in when you are trying to get into the main stream of traffic from a side road; the game seems to be to see how many drivers you can block! Cutting close in front is another favourite game.

Consequently the police have a big job to keep an eye on traffic offences. Drink drivers have recently been blitzed by the police department, with road blocks to check on drunks, who are then asked to blow into a little bag; if the crystals in the tube change colour, they can tell roughly how much drink has been consumed.

The penal system

New Zealand's penal system has evolved to protect the community from offenders both through deterrence and reformation, with increasing emphasis on rehabilitation in recent years.

The main sources available to the courts for dealing with offenders, other than by imprisonment, are fines, reparation, supervision, community services, periodic detention and community care. On conviction for murder a mandatory sentence of life imprisonment is imposed. The death penalty for murder was abolished in 1961. Capital punishment was removed as a penalty for all crimes (latterly treason and mutiny in the armed forces) in 1989.

The most common violent offences by males receiving custodial sentences were aggravated robbery (18% of violent offenders and 9% of all prison inmates) and injuring and wounding (13% of violent offenders and 7% of all inmates).

The most significant major offence groups represented for

females were property offences (40%) and violent offences (34%). A smaller proportion of female prisoners were incarcerated for drug offences (16%) and six females were in custody for traffic offences. The most common violent offences for which female offenders were given custodial sentences were murder (25% of all violent offenders and 8% of all inmates) and injuring and wounding (26% of violent offenders and 8% of all inmates).

Nearly half (48%) of the cases which resulted in a custodial sentence for some offence other than a traffic offence related to Maori offenders, 43% to European offenders and 7% to Pacific Islanders, according to the New Zealand Statistics Department.

The police
On 1 July 1992 the New Zealand Police and the Ministry Transport's Traffic Safety Service merged to concentrate resources and target serious traffic offences.

The national administrative and operational control of the New Zealand Police is vested in a commissioner who is responsible to the Government through the Minister of Police. For operational purposes, New Zealand is divided into six police regions, each controlled by an assistant commissioner.

Regional commanders are responsible for the general preservation of peace and order, for the prevention of offences, and for the detection of offenders in their areas of command. Policing is maintained by a system of mobile patrols and foot 'beats', coordinated by communications network.

The police are responsible for enforcing the criminal law principally the **Crimes Act** and the **Summary Offences Act**, but also various other statutes such as the **Arms Act**, **Sale of Liquor Act**, **Gaming and Lotteries Act**, **Misuse of Drugs Act** and **Transport Act**.

The summary prosecution of criminal offences investigated by the police is undertaken in the District Court by trained police prosecutors. Police in country districts in some cases hold additional appointments such as registrars and bailiffs at District Courts, probation officers and honorary fishery officers.

The ordinary police are not armed. The **armed offenders squads** are a group of specially equipped and trained officers who deal with offenders with weapons. About 200 members throughout the country perform armed offenders squad duties on a part-time basis.

The **special tactics group** is made up of selected members of armed offenders squads who are specially trained to deal with any acts of terrorism. The only act of terrorism in New Zealand was in

1985 when a team of French saboteurs entered the country illegally by sea.

'The Rainbow Warrior' – 10 July 1985
On a peaceful winter's night in July 1985, two frogmen slipped into the cold waters of Auckland Harbour. They attached two explosives to the hull of *The Rainbow Warrior*, the flagship of Greenpeace, and hurried away.

There was a party on board, a birthday celebration attended by 30 people. The first explosion was felt and lights went out and the ship started to list, everyone got off the ship except for the photographer Fernando Pereira; he decided that he had time to rescue his camera equipment. The second explosion came, and the ship went down with Fernando.

LAW FOR DRIVERS

These are some key New Zealand laws to know:

- The legal drinking age is 20 years of age.
- Traffic travels on the left-hand side of the road.
- Cyclists must wear safety helmets.
- Motorcyclists must wear crash helmets and always display their lights.
- The wearing of seat belts in vehicles is compulsory.
- Speed limits: 100 km/h for cars, motorcycles, vans and light vehicles; 90 km/h for buses, heavy motor and articulated vehicles; 80 km/h for school buses and any vehicles towing trailers.

The major cause of accidents on the roads is excess alcohol and exceeding the speed limit.

Vehicle inspections
All vehicles using the roads must be inspected regularly to ensure their mechanical and structural fitness. They are inspected every six months, but vehicles first registered since 1 December 1985 and less than three years of age may be inspected every twelve months. Most lightweight vehicles are required to have a 'Warrant of Fitness'

which can be issued at approved garages or at Testing Stations.

Old-fashioned courtesies

Petrol stations in New Zealand are very much serve yourself, but you can still get service. I was astonished whilst on a trip to England recently to find that my dear old Mum, who is in her 80s, had to fill up her own car with petrol.

Importing your car

There are costs involved in bringing your car into New Zealand, and these costs depend mainly on the country in which your car was manufactured.

- If, for instance, your car was manufactured in the United Kingdom you will be charged a duty based on the price paid for that car of 20 per cent (less depreciation).

- For cars manufactured in any other country, there will be a duty based on the price you paid for the car, less depreciation, of 35 per cent.

- First time immigrants will *not* be charged duty if they have owned the car for twelve months before coming to New Zealand.

In some circumstances – even with the depreciation formula being applied – this valuation based on price paid will make the all-up cost of the vehicle to the importer thousands of dollars higher than the equivalent used vehicle in New Zealand. This situation is related to the reduction of car prices as a result of large numbers of secondhand cars being imported into New Zealand.

Collectors of Customs have authority to apply a method of valuation based upon the New Zealand market price of the vehicle where it can be established that the normal method of valuation will result in a substantial disadvantage to the importer.

This information is only a guide, and confirmation should be sought two to three months before shipping, by writing to:

The Collector of Customs –

PO Box 29, Manurewa, Auckland 1730. Tel: 64-9-275 1970.
PO Box 2218, Wellington 6015. Tel: 64-4-473 6099.
PO Box 440, Napier 4015. Tel: 64-6-835 5799.

Popular new car prices (approx.) all inclusive of GST (12.5%)

Alfa Romeo 146 1.6l TS	$37,995	Land Rover Defender 90	$53,800
Audi A3 1.8 Turbo	$54,900	Mazda 323 Astina Ltd	$29,195
BMW 318is Convertible	$82,000	Mercedes Benz E240 Classic	$103,700
Chrysler Neon LX	$28,490	MGF VVC	$59,000
Citroen Xsara 1.8 SX	$36,500	Mitsubishi L200 Petrol	$28,450
Daewoo Nubira SE	$25,500	Musso E32 Petrol	$51,040
Daihatsu Charade LsiA	$18,800	Nissan Pulsar LX Hatch	$27,195
Fiat Bravo 1.6SX	$27,995	Peugeot 406 VS	$63,000
Ford Mondeo LX 1.8 TDS	$31,900	Porsche 911 Carrera Coupé	$208,000
Holden Vectra GL 2.2 Sedan	$32,995	Renault Laguna 2.2 TD RXE	$50,000
Honda Prelude Vti-R	$42,000	Rover 416 Sli	$36,500
Honda Civic Lxi	$27,000	Saab 9-3 SE 2.0 Turbo	$67,200
Hyundai Lantra 1.6 GLS	$28,900	Subaru Impreza WRX 2.0	$46,990
Jaguar Sovereign 4.0 V8	$155,000	Suzuki Baleno GS	$18,950
Jeep Wrangler Spt Htop	$41,990	Toyota Starlet XL Hatch	$48,990
Kia Sportage 2.0 4WD DLX	$32,995	VW Passat 1.8	$69,950
Lada Niva 4WD	$14,495		

Petrol prices in New Zealand are approximately $1.12 per litre for unleaded petrol.

Secondhand car prices (approx.)
Here are some typical examples:

1992 Alfa Romeo 33S P4WD	$17,000	1994 Mercedes Benz C280	$39,995
1997 Audi A4 Quattro turbo	$37,995	1993 Mitsubishi Galant Viento	$14,999
1992 BMW 535i	$29,990	1994 Nissan Sunny Salon	$13,999
1993 Citroen Xantia 2.0i	$18,000	1991 Peugeot 205 Gti	$15,000
1994 Daihatsu Charade hatch	$8,999	1992 Porsche 928 GTS	$79,999
1995 Fiat Punto turbo	$15,990	1996 Renault Laguna	$25,999
1992 Ford Laser XL 1.6	$6,995	1990 Range Rover Vogue SE	$25,999
1991 Holden Commodore	$15,990	1994 Saab 900S	$23,999
1991 Honda Accord Ascot	$11,999	1998 Subaru Legacy	$19,999
1995 Hyundai Sonata 3.0 V6	$16,499	1992 Suzuki Alto	$6,995
1990 Jaguar xj40 Sovereign	$34,995	1993 Toyota Corona	$14,999
1995 Land Rover Discovery	$32,990	1994 VW Golf	$20,990
1995 Mazda Lantis X 5dr	$18,995	1992 Volvo 940 GL	$16,999

Those are just a few advertisements taken at random. If you would like to see more, write to one of the newspaper offices and ask for a current issue to be sent to you.

The New Zealand Herald, Box 32, Auckland.
The Dominion, Box 1297, Wellington.
The Otago Times, Box 517, Dunedin.
The Christchurch Star, Box 1467, Christchurch.

The cost of one newspaper to the United Kingdom would be about NZ$12.55 airmail and $4.05 sea mail. Send your money with your request; payments may be made by cheque or credit card.

New intending residents
An immigrant, *ie* a person coming to New Zealand to take up permanent residence for the first time, is allowed duty and GST free entry of a motor vehicle, motorcycle and motor scooter under the conditions set out below. It is possible for more than one vehicle to qualify under this concession. To benefit you must be able to comply with all of the following requirements, supported by full documentary evidence:

- You are coming for the first time to New Zealand to take up permanent residence (that is, you have never lived in New Zealand).

- You must have personally owned and personally used the vehicle for at least one year before the date of your departure for New Zealand or the date on which the vehicle is surrendered for shipping, whichever is the earlier.

- You must be importing the vehicle for your own personal use and not for sale, gift or disposal in any other way.

- You must be prepared to give a written undertaking that if you sell or dispose of the vehicle within two years of the date of its importation, you will pay an amount equal to the duty and GST which would otherwise be payable.

The terms of the above concessions are legal requirements as set out in the Tariff of New Zealand. Unless you can satisfy the Customs that all these requirements have been complied with, full duty and GST will be payable. If you require an assessment of the amount of duty and GST payable on your car, please obtain a copy of Customs Notice No. Six. *Private Motor Vehicle Imports.* This Notice explains how you should calculate the value for duty and how to determine the charges payable on the vehicle.

Steam cleaning
The Ministry of Agriculture and Fisheries require that all used vehicles entering New Zealand are steam cleaned to prevent the introduction of animal and plant diseases and pests, except used vehicles from Australia if on inspection at the port of entry they are

found to be clean.

To avoid delay in New Zealand, vehicles may be steam cleaned immediately prior to shipment and a **Certificate of Steam Cleaning** produced to the Agriculture Quarantine Service on arrival. An inspection of the vehicle is required before release to ensure that cleaning has been adequate. This will be carried out at an approved area.

Vehicles not steam cleaned before loading, or found to be contaminated on arrival, will be cleaned in New Zealand and reinspected before release. The cost of having your car steam cleaned here is approximately NZ\$44 which includes Goods and Services Tax.

We shipped our car out to New Zealand – it took approximately five weeks to arrive.

Left-hand drive vehicles
Under the Customs Import Prohibition Order (No. Two) 1952, there is a restriction on the importation of left-hand drive vehicles. Before shipping a left-hand drive vehicle to New Zealand you must obtain approval to import from the Ministry of Transport, Land Transport Division, 1 Queen Street, Private Bag 106 602, New Zealand. Tel: 64-0800 108 809.

Registration and licensing of vehicles
All vehicles using public roads need to be registered six monthly:

Vehicle	*Annual fee (approx.)*
Cars	\$107.30
Motorcycles	\$ 94.70 (60cc or less)
	\$135.00 (over 60cc)
Rental cars	\$120.05
Vans	\$107.30
Tractors (non road use)	\$ 21.30

Note: for further details about registration in New Zealand: E-mail: *info@tregistry.co.nz*.

The 'infernal' combustion engine
Cars are one of the biggest threats to the global environment. The transport sector is estimated to be responsible for 40% of New Zealand's greenhouse gas emissions. New Zealand has the second highest rate of cars per capita in the world, with petrol consumption

NEW ZEALAND

MINISTRY OF TRANSPORT

LICENCE NUMBER

This **LICENCE** to drive a motor vehicle is issued by the Secretary for Transport and is valid for the following class/es:

Signature of Licence Holder: _____

(Licence not valid till signed)

Issued to:

Date of Birth:

Eye Colour:

Date of Issue:

Expiry Date:

SPECIAL CONDITIONS:

(SEE REVERSE FOR CODING)

Fig. 24. A New Zealand driving licence.

increasing by 4% a year. Because of the relatively small population and spread of the towns and cities, it is not always possible to use public transport, hence the high use of private vehicles.

GETTING THROUGH CUSTOMS & EXCISE

New Zealand is relatively free of pests and beasties, and intends to keep it that way! Its geographical isolation has provided a natural barrier against many of the world's more serious agricultural pests and diseases. Strict quarantine laws are in place to prevent this, and are enforced by uniformed officers who carry out inspections at seaports and airports.

There are heavy penalties for concealing dutiable goods from customs, for making false declarations, and for presenting false documentation such as false receipts.

People who knowingly bring restricted items into New Zealand and do not declare them will be prosecuted and will be subject to severe penalties and forfeit of goods.

Prepare to be checked

If you are bringing camping gear, tramping shoes, farm work clothing *etc* you must declare these to the MAF people at the

Customs counter at the airport. They can then be carefully inspected to ensure they are free from any harmful substances.

Only recently two Russian cargo ships were suspected of carrying Asian gypsy moth eggs, which would have been laid whilst the ship was in an overseas port. The MAF had to inspect every inch of one of the vessels where some eggs were found on a packing case, and the other ship was not allowed into New Zealand ports because it wasn't considered to be 'clean'. If the eggs got into New Zealand they would very rapidly establish themselves in this country; since there are 'ideal' breeding conditions, these moths could devastate New Zealand's forests.

You might think there would be no harm in bringing in your favourite pot of jam or honey, a cutting from your special rose bush, and you might even think that your family goldfish wouldn't cause a tragedy. It would – **these things would be destroyed on your arrival**. So why not find them a good home *before* you leave? The same applies to the cat and the canary – *don't* think you can smuggle them in.

Prohibited goods
The following are prohibited, and you will need special **CITES certification** to bring them into New Zealand:

- Ivory in any form, that includes jewellery, ornaments *etc*.

- Eggs and egg products, dried egg powder, instant meal products and egg cartons.

- Freshwater fish including salmon and trout, except canned.

- Honey including pollen, honeycombs, beeswax.

- Meat and meat products, fresh or cooked, including small goods except canned products.

- Popcorn (unpopped).

- Leis and Lei materials (Pacific island garlands).

- Plants live, dried, including pot plants and plant cuttings (except with correct certification).

- Straw packaging. Straw handcrafts may be allowed after examination and treatment.

- Animals, domestic pets, birds, fish, insects and fertilised eggs.

- Biological cultures and organisms.
- Clam shells and coral in any form, including jewellery, curios and souvenirs.
- Turtle and tortoise shells, including jewellery, souvenirs, hand crafts and curios.

Restricted goods
The following items are restricted and *must* be declared on arrival, when they will be examined:

- Coconuts including unprocessed product and husks.
- Dairy products, cheeses, milk, milk powder, butter, milk-based baby foods.
- Saltwater fish, fresh, dried and frozen, all species.
- Fruit, fresh, dried, frozen or cooked.
- Herbs and spices in any form, including when used in medicines.
- Honey from Niue.
- Mushrooms, fresh or dried.
- Noodles and rice including processed and instant meal products.
- Nuts, unprocessed and raw.
- Vegetables, fresh, dried, frozen or cooked.
- Bamboo, cane, rattan, basketware and mats in any form.
- Bulbs, corms, rhizomes and tubers.
- Cut flowers, dried flowers and leaves.
- Pine cones and pot pourri, including natural and decorative products.
- Seeds in any form including commercially packaged.
- Animal remedies, including vaccines, pet and stock foods.
- Artefacts including wooden carvings, figurines, shields, drums spears and masks.
- Camping equipment including clothing and footwear.
- Clothing, equipment and footwear used on farms or where animals are present (including slaughter houses) and shearing equipment.

- Feathers, bones, horns and tusks in any form.

- Furs, skins and hunting trophies.

- Saddles and riding equipment including clothing, footwear and grooming equipment.

- Soil and water in any form, including religious items.

- Stuffed animals and reptiles.

- Wool (unprocessed) and animal hair, including yarns, crafted rugs and apparel.

Remember, by complying with these regulations you are helping New Zealand to protect its $8 billion horticultural industries which could be devastated by dangerous pests and diseases.

All fresh fruit, vegetables and living plant matter *must* have an **International Phytosanitary Certificate** (IPC) before they can be brought into New Zealand. Such goods arriving without the necessary documents will be destroyed or shipped to their country of origin at the passenger's expense.

For further clarification on these matters, you could contact the New Zealand Immigration Office or Embassy nearest to you, or contact:

The Ministry of Agriculture & Fisheries, Ray Emery Drive, Mangere, Auckland 1701. Tel: 64-9-275 5668.

The Ministry of Agriculture & Fisheries, Box 2526, Wellington 6001. Tel: 64-4-472 0367.

The Ministry of Agriculture & Fisheries, Box 54, Kaitaia 0500. Tel: 64-09-408 0900.

Bringing in animals

If you are from the United Kingdom, Norway, Sweden, Hawaii or Australia, and your dog or cat has been born in that country, then there are no quarantine requirements, only health tests which must be done before coming to New Zealand.

If, however, you are from a country other than the above, then there are strict quarantine requirements. Your animal will have to be quarantined in England for six months plus two months residency, or in Hawaii for four months, with two months residency, before being allowed into New Zealand. For further clarification or any further queries please contact one of the Ministry of Agriculture and Fisheries offices given above.

Bringing in drugs

Do not import drugs into New Zealand. The importation of drugs could result in your imprisonment. Be extremely wary of carrying packages or baggage for strangers.

QUESTIONS AND ANSWERS

What protection is there for a potential secondhand car buyer?

A motor vehicle securities register is administered by the Department of Justice; this is called **Autocheck**. A consumer considering buying a vehicle can phone the register toll free to check if any security interest is registered against the vehicle.

Can I drive in New Zealand on an overseas licence?

A valid driver's licence can be used for one year in New Zealand; the owner must then take a written and oral test in order to obtain a New Zealand driver's licence.

8

The Government and the Economy

NEW ZEALAND'S CONSTITUTION

New Zealand's constitutional history can be traced back to 1840. Under the Treaty of Waitangi, the Maori people exchanged their sovereignty for the guarantees of the treaty and New Zealand became a British colony. New Zealand is today an independent state, a monarchy with a parliamentary government. Queen Elizabeth II has the title of Queen of New Zealand.

The constitution is concerned with the legislative, executive and judicial organs of government, their composition, powers and duties, and the relationship of these organs. New Zealand's Constitution Act 1986 brings together in one statute the most important provisions and clarifies the rules relating to the governmental handover of power. It deals with the main components of New Zealand's statutory constitutional provisions: the Sovereign, the executive, the legislature and the judiciary. The Act and its provisions are safeguarded by the requirement of a special procedure to make amendments. The Electoral Act 1956 is the only other New Zealand constitutional statute to have such a provision.

A number of United Kingdom Acts (referred to as 'Imperial Acts') are still in force as part of the law of New Zealand. Some are historic constitutional Acts, such as the Magna Carta and the Habeas Corpus Act 1679. These Acts are listed and defined in the Imperial Laws' Application Act 1988.

A parliamentary monarchy

A British colony since 1840, national sovereignty was established by the Statute of Westminster in 1947; however, New Zealand remains a monarchy. The Governor-General, Queen Elizabeth II's representative, summons and dissolves Parliament, and assents to legislation.

The Parliament is made up of 120 members of the House of

Representatives, elected under a mixed member proportional (MMP) voting system. General elections are held every three years.

National leaders

Governor-General	His Excellency Rt Hon Sir Paul Reeves
Prime Minister	Rt Hon Helen Clark
Deputy Prime Minister	Hon Jim Anderton
Leader of the Opposition	Rt Hon Jenny Shipley

The seat of Government is the **Beehive**, situated in Central Wellington, the capital of New Zealand.

The Maoris
The Treaty of Waitangi
The **hapu** and **iwi** are the indigenous tribes and sub-tribes of New Zealand and their peoples now comprise about 14.5% of the population. In 1840 they signed a compact agreeing to exchange their governance for the guarantees of the Treaty of Waitangi. This treaty established the modern nation of New Zealand.

While the treaty has always been recognised and valued within Maori society, it could not be enforced in the courts as it has never been incorporated into statute law. In a landmark Court of Appeal case (*New Zealand Maori Council v Attorney General, 1987*) the special relationship between the Maori people and the Crown was interpreted by the Court as requiring the partners to act reasonably and with the utmost good faith towards each other. A number of Acts of Parliament now require the Crown to have regard to the principles of the Treaty of Waitangi, or to Maori interests or a Maori perspective.

Waitangi Tribunal
This tribunal considers claims from any Maori who considers he or she, or any group of Maori of which he or she is a member, is prejudiced by any legislation, policy or practice by or on behalf of the Crown which is inconsistent with the principles of the Treaty of Waitangi.

In the year 1991–92 the major report completed was that concerning the Te Roroa claim in the Dargaville area. Beginning 30 June 1992 hearings and conferences were held on 17 claims. Some of the areas under examination were the Ngai Tahu fisheries, Crown Forest assets; Tainui (Waikato River dam); railway lands; geothermal claims; Waikareao Estuary and Wellington Tenths.

The Crown and the Governor-General

The Governor-General is the representative of the Sovereign in New Zealand and exercises the royal powers derived from statute and the general law (prerogative powers). The powers of the Governor-General are set out in the Letters Patent 1983, and it is for the courts to decide on the limits of these powers. The Governor-General's main role is to arrange for the leader of the majority party in Parliament to form a government. Almost all the powers of the Governor-General are now statutory.

The Crown is part of Parliament and so the Governor-General's assent is required before bills can become law. The Governor-General is required, however, by constitutional convention and by the Letters Patent, to follow the advice of ministers. In extra-ordinary circumstances the Governor-General can reject advice if he or she believes that a government is intending to act unconstitutionally. This is known as the 'reserve power'.

The Sovereign appoints the Governor-General on the Prime Minister's recommendation, normally for a term of five years.

How Parliament works

Parliament consists of the Sovereign and House of Representatives. The members of the House, which has one chamber, are elected by universal suffrage in accordance with the Electoral Act 1956. Each Parliament has a term of three years, unless dissolved earlier. The Governor-General has the power to summon, discontinue and dissolve Parliament. The Queen and the Governor-General act on the advice of their Ministers.

The Constitution Act provides for Parliament to have full power to make laws; a Bill passed by the House becomes law when the Sovereign or Governor-General assents to it. The Act cancels the power of the United Kingdom Parliament to make laws for New Zealand.

The Constitution Act reaffirms the constitutional principles about parliamentary control of public finance; the Crown may not levy taxes, raise loans, or spend public money except through an Act of Parliament.

The judiciary

The judiciary is the third branch of government. The Constitution Act includes mechanisms to preserve the independence of judges, an important principle of the New Zealand Constitution. The judiciary interprets Acts passed by Parliament and also reviews actions of the

Executive to ensure that it is acting within the law.

New Zealand Bill of Rights 1990
New Zealand has a Bill of Rights, but the Act of 1990 is not entrenched as 'higher law'. Thus the judiciary cannot strike down laws which are inconsistent with it. Where a legal provision is ambiguous, the Courts are required to interpret that provision consistently with the rights and freedoms contained in the Bill of Rights Act.

The Bill of Rights defines basic human rights. It applies to actions of the legislative, executive and judicial branches of government and to the activities of the public services.

Other sources of the Constitution
Included among other sources of the Constitution are the prerogative powers of the Sovereign, other statutes such as the State Sector Act 1988, the Electoral Act 1956 and the Judicature Act 1908, relevant English and United Kingdom statutes as defined in the Imperial Laws Application Act 1988, decisions of the Courts and conventions such as the democratic nature of the New Zealand constitution.

Political parties
There are two dominant political parties, the National and Labour parties. The Labour Party formed the Government between 1984 and October 1990, and the National Party from October 1990 until the elections of late 1993. In the 1993 general election when the National Party was returned people were not only asked to vote for their member of parliament, but whether or not they favoured MMP (mixed member proportional) system rather than the FPP (first past the post) system. The MMP won by a small margin. At the next election in 1996 parliamentary members were elected by MMP. Third parties have also been elected to Parliament in recent years in very small numbers, and a few members have left the main political parties to sit as independents.

Public service
The state sector is responsible for carrying out the policies of the government. It comprises government departments and ministries along with the parliamentary, education, social welfare, housing, health and defence services, and a number of statutory organisations. The role of the public service is defined in the State Sector Act

1988, the Public Finance Act 1989 and the Official Information Act 1982, as well as in a large number of specific statutes.

Voting in elections

Persons 18 years and over have the right to vote in parliamentary elections. Enrolment as an elector is compulsory, but voting is not. To qualify for enrolment persons must:

● be at least 18 years old

● be New Zealand citizens or New Zealand residents

● have lived continuously in New Zealand for at least a year at some time

● have lived continuously for one month in the electorate they are to be enrolled in.

The conduct of polls is the responsibility of the Department of Justice. It is controlled by a returning officer in each electorate, who arranges voting facilities and staff, conducts the election, supervises the counting of votes, and declares the result.

Voting is by secret ballot. A preliminary count of ordinary votes is available for each electorate on election night, and final results are normally available a fortnight later, once special overseas votes have been received and counted. But the outcome of the voting is generally clear by the following day.

A CHANGING ECONOMY

Despite the problems of being a small population separated by a tremendous distance from most of the rest of the world's population, New Zealand has become a significant trading economy. The trade has always been based on farming, but in recent years New Zealand has been forced to diversify its markets and products. At present Australia is its largest export market, followed by Japan, the United States of America and the United Kingdom.

An exporting nation

New Zealand depends much on its export earnings. The following list summarises its key export business:

Principal exports	1998 $(m)	1999 $(m)
Meat & edible offal	2,928	2,830
Fish, crustaceans & molluscs	1,027	1,158
Milk powder, butter & cheese	3,729	4,005
Wood & wood articles	1,557	1,408
Aluminium & articles thereof	990	1,045
Wool	933	797
Fruit and nuts	837	894
Casein & caseinates	624	699
Electrical machinery	645	699
Raw hides, skins, leather	635	560
Principal imports		
Mechanical machinery	3,147	3,414
Vehicles, parts and accessories	2,299	2,785
Electrical machinery	2,315	2,430
Textiles and textile articles	1,332	1,364
Mineral fuels	1,420	1,355
Plastic and plastic articles	958	993
Aircraft and parts	447	862
Optical, medical equipment	725	759

Export oddities

The Government has been promoting a drive for an export-led economic recovery, and this has led to many New Zealand businesses developing new and unique overseas trade opportunities. The following are a few of the more enterprising examples taken from information published by the Department of Statistics:

- Seagram (NZ) Ltd are providing South Korea with 100,000 litres of malt whisky from its Dunedin-based Wilsons distillery.

- Hills Hats Ltd in Porirua won a contract to supply 36,000 woollen berets to the United Nations Peace Keeping forces.

- Orange roughy fish roe, once a waste product of orange roughy processing, is being marketed by a Wellington firm as an alternative to caviar. It has been successfully tried out in restaurants and will soon be available on Air New Zealand flights. Companies in New York, Sydney and Melbourne are interested in importing the roe which compares favourably with Russian lumpfish roe at a fraction of the price.

- Suttons Moss Ltd on the West Coast is exporting $1 million worth of sphagnum moss to Japan and Taiwan.

- Southern Alpsocks, manufacturers of outdoor socks, sold a consignment of 5,000 pairs to a Canadian outdoors wear chain. The firm said that New Zealand outdoor wear products had a high reputation in Canada and that they plan to use the socks' origin as a selling point.

- Deer velvet exports for 1991 topped $50m, mostly to South-east Asia.

- Trial exports of opossum meat to Taiwan and Hong Kong have proven promising. If trade takes off, a return of $10 per carcass is expected.

- Tikaland Products have developed small but thriving niche markets in Australia, Britain and Germany for their canvas backpacks and cycle panniers.

- Riverland Estate Winery in the Kumeu valley supplied 120,000 bottles of sparkling kiwifruit wine to an importer in Florida. The wine is like an Asti but drier, suiting the American palate for dry wines.

- A Palmerston North entrepreneur is importing live ostriches for farming in New Zealand. Ostriches produce edible meat, feathers, oils for cosmetics, and soft leather suitable for making bags and leisure wear. The birds will be slaughtered in New Zealand and sent overseas for processing.

- Earnest Adams Ltd made an initial export sale of 54,000 microwave pies to supply 500 supermarkets throughout Taiwan. The mince and beefsteak pies are the first of the type available in Taiwan.

- Christchurch boat-engine manufacturer CWF Hamilton received an order for six twin jet engines to power rescue boats for the Italian Coast Guard.

- The largest-ever shipment of hydrogen peroxide, 800 tonnes valued at $1m and manufactured by Du Pont New Zealand, was exported to South America.

Agriculture
Farming and horticulture are major industries, providing a high proportion of New Zealand's export earnings. Traditionally farming

has centred on sheep and cattle to produce sheepmeat, beef, wool, dairy produce and hides, although in recent years new types of livestock have included deer, goats and fur bearing animals such as fitch.

Horticulture has always provided well for the home market, but since the 1970s horticultural produce has become an important export earner.

Meat

Meat industry products are New Zealand's second largest export income earner, accounting for about 18% of merchandise exports. New Zealand's main meat exports are lamb, mutton and beef. About 80% of these products in 1997–98 were exported overseas. The domestic market purchases over 99% of the pigmeat and poultry produced in New Zealand.

Export marketing

New Zealand is a major exporter of sheepmeat, accounting for 54% of the world export trade; it is a small player in the global market for beef, accounting for about 6.4% of all the world beef exports.

New Zealand's major meat markets include the United Kingdom, Germany, France, Saudi Arabia and the United States for lamb; the United Kingdom, South Korea and France for mutton; and the United States, Canada, Japan, South Korea and Taiwan for beef.

Wool

New Zealand sheep are largely dual purpose meat/wool animals and their wool is predominantly strong; 75% of the clip is greater than 33 microns in diameter. This contrasts sharply with Australian wool, of which 99% is less than 33 microns. New Zealand is by far the largest producer of strong wools: it contributes a quarter of the world total and two and a half times as much as either the former Soviet Union or China, the next most significant producers. When the quantity of strong wool entering world trade is considered, New Zealand's share becomes even greater. Over 70% of traded strong wools are estimated to originate in New Zealand.

Net domestic consumption of wool in New Zealand is amongst the highest in the world on a per head basis. In 1997–98 the largest importers of New Zealand wool were China, the United Kingdom, India, Germany and Belgium.

New Zealanders love to luxuriate in pure wool products; the babies lie on pure sheepskin rugs, and customers look for the 'Pure

New Zealand Wool' labels when purchasing clothing. Beds often have pure sheepskin underlays, and pure wool blankets. The shops and offices usually have wall to wall carpets, and so of course do private homes.

Wool product exports
The most important wool product exports from New Zealand are floor coverings and yarns. It is estimated that 34% of New Zealand wool is used in machine-made carpets, 12% in handknotted and hand-tufted carpets, 44% in apparel, and 10% in other uses, primarily upholstery and bedding. Total export earnings from wool products were $25.5 million in 1997–98.

Dairy produce
Dairy product exports constitute over 20% of total merchandise trade receipts for New Zealand, and, with the exception of milk and some dairy products for local consumption, the industry is primarily geared towards overseas markets – which account for between 90 and 95% of all milk produced on an annual basis.

Overseas marketing
The international market for dairy products is characterised by its small size relative to total world milk production, with only about 5% of production entering international trade. Because of this the market is especially vulnerable to shifts in climatic, commercial and political forces. Marginal production changes in the major producers can trigger massive shifts in supplies of, and prices for, products on the international market.

The major dairy exporters are the European Union, New Zealand, Australia, and to a lesser degree the United States of America and Canada. These five exporters supply between 90 and 95% of dairy products traded on the international market. Relatively smaller quantities are exported by the Nordic countries and from Eastern Europe.

The dairy industry has been working to diversify its markets for many years. Today, New Zealand's major markets vary for different products. There has been reduced access to both the United Kingdom and the European Union butter market; Britain, however, remains New Zealand's most valuable market for butter.

The old Soviet Union countries are important purchasers of New Zealand butter, as is the Middle East and North Africa, both of which have recently risen to prominence as markets for New

Zealand produce.

The Dairy Board's export earnings from dairy products in 1998 were $4.6 billion, over 20% of total New Zealand merchandise exports.

Grape growing and wine production

The major grape growing regions are Gisborne, Hawkes Bay, Marlborough, Auckland and Poverty Bay. Perhaps you may have seen these names on wine labels at your own supermarket.

In 1998 an estimated 7,356 ha were planted in producing grape vines. According to *Statistics New Zealand*, in 1998 exports of wine increased from 13.072 million litres in 1997 to 15.153 million litres.

In 1998, 78,300 tonnes of grapes were produced making it New Zealand's largest wine vintage to date. The most popular grapes of the season were: Chardonnay, 18,169 tonnes, Sauvignon Blanc, 15,136 tonnes and Muller Thurgau, 10,579 tonnes.

New Zealand's largest export market currently is the United Kingdom with 7.997 million litres of wine imported in the 1998 season. The second largest export market is Australia.

New Zealand has the most southerly vineyard in the world. Hawke's Bay is the first vineyard in the world to see the sun each day, because it is the area of New Zealand which is closest to the International Date Line.

Jane Hunter and Hunter's Wines

Leading international viticulturist and managing director of Hunter's Wines (NZ) Ltd, Jane Hunter has successfully led Hunter's Wines since the death of her husband Ernie Hunter in 1987. Jane grew up in the Riverland area of South Australia where her parents owned vineyards. Jane married Ernie Hunter, an Irish immigrant, in 1984. Ernie had pioneered the overseas marketing and promotion of New Zealand wines and had established Hunter's Wines at Blenheim in the early 1980s.

Since taking over Hunter's Wines, Jane has expanded the winery's operations – 40,000 cases of wine are now produced annually, three times the amount produced in 1987. Twenty per cent of the winery's produce is exported to Britain, Ireland, Switzerland, Canada and Australia.

Hunter's wines have earned an international reputation. Jane Hunter has been billed as one of the five best female 'wine makers' in the world, and her wines have been requested by the King of Sweden and the Prince of Thailand. The winery has won many international awards ranging from number one chardonnay in the world for its 1986 vintage, to the 1991 sauvignon blanc being awarded the Marquis de Goulaine trophy for the best in its class at the 1992 London International Wine and Spirit Competition. More recently the winery has concentrated on producing dry white wines and promising red wines. If you haven't done so already, try some!

Forestry

Forests cover about 29% or 8.1m hectares of New Zealand's land area. Of this about 6.4 million hectares are in natural forest and the rest is planted in production forest. Of the total planted production estate, about 91% is radiata pine (pinus radiata) and 5% douglas fir. Hardwoods comprise about 3% of New Zealand's planted production forests. The most important hardwood plantation species are eucalyptus originating from Australia.

Many of the earlier plantation forests were developed by the state, but the impetus for development and ownership has moved increasingly to the private sector over recent decades as the industry's capital and infrastructure has expanded. This has led to the planting of 52,000 hectares of new forest in 1998. The volume of wood available for export is expected to increase dramatically, with about a 74% increase between 1996 and 2010. This projected increase assumes 60,000 hectares of new plantings occur each year.

Exports

Forest products are important earners of overseas funds. For the year to June 1998 exports of forest products were valued at about NZ$2,242m. Australia was the largest customer, taking 31%, mainly in sawn timber, paper and paperboard, panel products and wood pulp. The rest is taken by smaller customers, of which the largest was Korea at 11%.

Fisheries

New Zealands 200 nautical mile Exclusive Economic Zone (EEZ) is, with an area of 1.3 million square nautical miles, one of the world's largest. There are about 1,000 species of marine fish known in these waters, of which about 100 are commercially significant.

For a number of years the Government has limited foreign fishing in New Zealand waters to the tuna fisheries. Foreign charter fleets used to dominate the deepwater fisheries. There has been a significant investment by the seafood industry in new vessels with 63% of the total catch been taken now by New Zealand vessels.

Exports
The New Zealand fishing industry is export orientated, with more than 80% of the commercial catch being sold overseas. Significant exports in 1997 were:

Commodity exported	Quantity tonnes (000)	Value NZ$m
Finfish or wetfish	261.6	746.1
Rock lobster	2.9	111.2
Shellfish	73.5	268.4

The principal export markets for 1998 were Japan, $283.4m, United States, $195.5m and Australia, $130.6m.

Energy and minerals
New Zealand depends on a sustained supply of energy and mineral resources to fuel the economy, maintain industry and commerce, and sustain the well-being of its citizens. New Zealand is not self-sufficient in a number of key energy and mineral commodities; the shortfall is made up by imports.

The importance of oil security was highlighted during the 1990–91 Gulf crisis, when measures were taken to boost local oil production. This was done in conjunction with International Energy Agency emergency procedures. While the crisis did result in price rises, these were not as great as in some other countries nor were there any problems with continuity of supply. International oil markets are now more flexible than they were in the 1970s, with less risk of major disruptions to imported oil supplies. Thus, while oil supply security is still an important issue, it is unlikely to be as crucial as it was in the 1970s.

Unless significant new oil and gas discoveries are made, New Zealand's long-term self-sufficiency in hydrocarbons is expected to decline after 2005 as known oil and gas reserves run down.

Electricity
New Zealand is fortunate to have many rivers suitable for generating cheap hydro power. Hydro electricity was first used in New Zealand in the gold mining industry and the first generating station supplying the public with electricity was installed in Reefton in 1887 by the Reefton Electric Lighting Co. The first general government operated station was the Lake Coleridge scheme opened in 1914. The first thermal station was Meremere which was opened in 1958.

The winter of 1992 was quite severe, with record snow falls, and hard frosts. Unfortunately the hydro lakes were also quite low after a dry summer and autumn, and so everyone was encouraged to 'switch off' – and even shower together! – to save electricity.

The possibility of 'wind power' is now being looked into as a real alternative to hydro. In Wellington recently, high on a hill overlooking the Harbour, a propeller was erected on top of a tall pole, to test the viability of wind power.

Natural gas

Almost a third of the gas produced in New Zealand is used by electric power stations at New Plymouth, Huntley and Stratford. Another third is used to produce synthetic petrol at Motunui and 13% goes to produce methanol at Wairata. Industrial and commercial users consume the rest. Not all areas can receive gas for residential use.

Geothermal energy

Geothermal steam is used for electricity generation in the Wairakei and Ohaaki geothermal power stations. It is also used for direct process industrial heating, and for commercial and household heating. Geothermal waters are also used for recreational purposes and tourism.

Although geothermal systems are found throughout New Zealand, only those in the area between Lake Taupo and the Bay of Plenty (15 high temperature fields), and in Northland (Ngawha field) have the potential to provide a significant energy resource.

Whilst travelling from Tauranga in the Bay of Plenty, to Lake Taupo, you will pass through Wairakei Thermal Area; you will see signs as you approach, warning you of the danger of steam blocking your visibility as you drive through. The children always used to play 'spot the geyser' and look for areas where steam would just be pouring out of the earth, as there are many such locations in the Taupo area. The sheer delight of plunging into a thermal 'hot pool' is something indescribable. There are several of these in commercial areas throughout the Bay of Plenty, Rotorua and Taupo areas. In Rotorua many of the motels have their own thermal hot pools.

Minerals

New Zealand's mineral resources are diverse, but mining is generally small scale. Gold, ironsand, clays and sand and gravel for construction are the main minerals mined. Total production of non-metallic minerals in 1991 was valued at about $208m, while the value of metallic minerals totalled about $5164m.

New Zealand has in the black sands of the west coast beaches a large potential resource, stretching from Westport in the South Island and from Wanganui to Muriwai in the North Island. New Zealand Steel Ltd has two mining operations in the North Island. Titanomagnetic slurry is pumped to ships moored offshore for export to Japan.

Manufacturing
Small firms make up a big slice of the manufacturing sector. In 1991 companies with fewer than 50 employees produced 85% of manufacturing output and represented two-thirds of the manufacturing workforce. Here is a quick overview:

Aluminium
New Zealand Aluminium Smelter Ltd's Tiwai Point smelter has an annual production capacity of 244,000 tonnes of ingots.

Chemicals
During 1992 a number of policies affecting the use of industrial chemicals were modified to give greater protection to the environment. Timber treatment chemicals such as PCP are no longer used in New Zealand, but their accumulation in and around major mills poses environmental problems.

Electronics
The main consumer products are whiteware, plus a few niche market products. Strong growth has been enjoyed in the agricultural technology, health, commercial/industrial and professional radio and communication sectors.

Engineering
The most significant contribution to growth in engineering has been the government's decision to commission two ANZAC frigates, in partnership with the Australian Government.

Motor vehicles and components
New Zealand no longer has a motor vehicle assembly industry. All vehicles are imported in a fully built-up state. Imports of popular cars include: Nissan, Ford, Mazda, Mitsubishi, Toyota and Honda.

Tyres
To protect the two tyre manufacturers in New Zealand there is a tariff levy of 15% on all imports.

Paper
The Kinleith Mill operated by NZFP Pulp & Paper Ltd produces kraft linerboard, sack kraft and market pulp. Most of this is destined for overseas markets.

Software
New Zealand software manufacturers are in the forefront of export growth. Concerted efforts are under way to increase software exports to Australia.

Carpets
The two main manufacturers which produce wool-rich carpets are Feltex Carpets and Cavalier Bremworth, both based in Auckland.

Footwear
New Zealand has a long established footwear manufacturing industry. In 1991 1 million pairs of shoes were exported, compared with 0.3 million pairs in 1986. Australia is the main destination of New Zealand footwear exports.

Assistance to industry
The Government's business development policy is aimed at assisting regions to identify and capitalise on their own opportunities for development. As part of this policy the Government provides targeted assistance through its **Business Development Programme**.

The object is to encourage businesses to become more innovative and internationally competitive. Currently the programme comprises a network of 21 Business Development Boards, three grant schemes, and the 'ExcelleNZ' quality products:

Business Development Board, Box 1041, Napier 4015. Tel: 64-6-835 2044.
Business Development Board, Box 7040, Auckland. Tel: 64-9-308 9141.
Business Development Board, Box 960, Hamilton 2015. Tel: 64-7-834 0100.

Business Development Board, Box 7045, Wanganui 5031.Tel: 64-6-
345 0949.

Beyond 2000

The shape of New Zealand society today, as in the past, is the
outcome of the interaction of global trends with uniquely local
circumstances. There have been strong, interconnected and highly
influential changes in the world that we live in. For example:

- awareness about globalisation, the effects that this places on the
  society, the economy and the government

- strengthening of the Information Technology industry which has
  provided new opportunities for both acquiring information and
  exploiting a global market

- shifts towards more service based businesses

- changes in export requirements from the diverse number of
  trading partners New Zealand now has.

Running alongside these significant economic alterations are
changes within New Zealand's social and demographic environ-
ments. These three factors all play a significant part in the shaping of
New Zealand's future.

Statistics have shown for over a decade that New Zealand has
been characterised as an aging population. However, New
Zealanders are also becoming more educated. The knowledge
economy may be creating more opportunities in employment for
those who are now involved in the education systems.

Globalisation will challenge the identity of New Zealanders. The
results could change current economic and social policies and
processes, blur international lines and characteristics and open up
networks and access to information.

The effects of these complex and interrelated changes on New
Zealand fall beyond the social and economic capital base, to impacts
on social and economic progress and well-being. As the Government
is in a current stage of change following the election of a new
Labour lead alliance, new polices and practices will soon come into
place. For a closer look at the changing economy go to the New
Zealand Immigration Service Website: *www.immigration.govt.nz*.

9

Women in New Zealand

THE STORY OF AN EARLY WOMAN SETTLER

According to family historian Anne Folkema, Jane Udy was pregnant with her fifth child when she landed on the beach at Te Whanganui a Tara (Port Nicholson) in February 1840.

Pito-one pa (Maori Meeting House) lay to the west; Hikoikoi was the mouth of the river estuary to the east, with the Waiwhetu Owhiti (Maori) settlements on the opposite bank. In between, assorted temporary dwellings housed the Europeans who had arrived on the ships *Aurora* and *Oriental.*

Jane Udy gave birth to Thomas Clemence on 25 May under an awning, hastily erected after the family's second cottage built of flax and grasses burnt to the ground.

Jane's husband Hart Udy was a builder, and was in great demand to build homes for the new settlers. It was said that there were only six builders in Wellington in 1840, so times were fruitful for Hart Udy and his family. His eldest son Hart Junior began working with him in 1844, when he was only nine. Jane Udy eventually became a mother of nine children, and ran the farm and home that they owned. Poultry and dairy products often contributed to household income, while other farm produce increased self-sufficiency. In this way the family built up sizeable savings.

However, the family's position in the Hutt Valley was not a straightforward one. Issues of land had not been settled, and in 1845 the Udys were stripped of their possessions by an unidentified Maori party.

In May 1846 a military outpost was attacked and six soldiers were killed. The Udys remained, hiding in the dense bush beside the river, or taking refuge in the Wesley Chapel.

Yes, the early settlers were a strong and determined breed. The women had to work long hard hours utilising what they could; they would have known 'luxuries' before they set sail for New Zealand, and upon arrival had to learn to live off the land and by their own wits.

When I came to New Zealand in 1972 things had settled down somewhat! I found the women very capable and able to turn their hand to just about anything.

I soon learned new skills, and find that I can now make a very good attempt at just about anything. I have learned how to bottle fruit, and can cook for any number of unexpected visitors, I can sew, having made several ball gowns, suits, dresses – you name it! I had always thought that Christmas mincemeat only came in jars off the shop shelf; upon coming to New Zealand I learned how to make my own mincemeat, and believe me I could put any bottling firm out of business if I so chose!

CENTENNIAL SUFFRAGE 1893–1993

Universal suffrage was gained in New Zealand in 1893, and the Government designated 1993 as Suffrage Centennial Year. It established a $5 million Trust Fund to contribute towards projects which will:

- enhance the status and advancement of women

- commemorate the centenary of women's suffrage in New Zealand

- publicise the positive contributions women have made to New Zealand's political, economic, social and cultural life.

The Trust's objectives are to stimulate activities which close the gaps between women and men, and Maori and non-Maori women, and to focus on projects which will help women achieve greater confidence, skills, opportunities and recognition.

In addition to community initiatives funded by the Trust and private sponsorship, all government departments will fund and organise activities and projects aimed at improving the situation of women.

A unit within the Ministry of Women's Affairs is servicing the Trust and coordinating centennial activities.

Women today

Women make up nearly 51% of the population and have adopted a saying, born out of television advertising, that 'girls can do anything'. Women can now be found in many job situations that only a few years ago would have been thought impossible.

- Lynne runs a haulage business in Auckland: she concentrates on house moving, and plays an equal role with her employees. She comments that other women's attitudes have been the hardest to take.

- Megan works as a 'melters tapper' at a steel mill in the South Island. Her working partner, a male, says that she is better than some of the men, and certainly more dependable in the dangerous job they do at the furnace face.

- Helen has worked as an overhead crane driver at a steel mill, doing the dangerous job of moving huge pots of molten metal from one spot to another. She says that she had to prove herself, and now the men respect her. It's a fine line she says; you mustn't be seen to be doing the job *too* well!

- Joan is a pilot with a commercial airline. She says that she has found most hostility from other women. One passenger was heard to say to her husband upon boarding the aircraft that she didn't fancy a woman driver!

- Carol has worked at a South Auckland Steel mill for six years as a crane driver. Initially she was ignored, but now she is accepted as one of the best.

- Women comprise 22% of the lawyers in New Zealand. They are generally paid less than men and fewer of them are partners in law firms.

- Racing is a big industry in New Zealand, with even the smallest of towns having race tracks. Only a few years ago it was a male dominated scene, but now half New Zealand jockeys are women!

- Penny Jamieson was the first woman to be consecrated as an Anglican bishop; the ceremony was performed in Dunedin in 1990.

- Dame Catherine Tizard was the first female Governor-General in New Zealand, a position she held from 1990 to 1996.

Status of New Zealand women 1992
The following is an extract from a report published by the Ministry of Women's Affairs.

Traditional occupations
'Women's increased numerical participation in the paid workforce has not been matched by across the board changes in the variety of occupations in which women are employed, or by the status of women within occupational groups. Women remain concentrated in a few industries and continue to work in traditional female occupations. Almost half of all employed women work in just six occupational groups – nurses, teachers, typists, bookkeepers/cashiers, clerical workers and sales assistants. Men heavily out-number women in the primary and secondary sectors of the economy (manufacturing, primary production, building and construction, mining *etc.*) Women significantly outnumber men in the service sector (community and personal services, wholesale and retail trade, restaurants and hotels, finance, insurance and real estate).

'Although gender differences in occupations remain marked, these are slowly being eroded. Accountancy, management and legal positions are examples of occupations where the proportion of women had risen dramatically to 15–25% by 1986. The proportion of economists who are women rose from 10% in 1971 to 35% in 1986. In each of the five occupations which contained the highest percentage of women in 1971, there were proportionately fewer women by 1986.

'Maori women demonstrate different employment patterns to non-Maori women, being more likely to be employed in production, transport, labouring and servicing occupations, and less likely to be working in professional and technical, administration and managerial, and sales and clerical occupations.'

Just as there are marked differences between occupations for men and women, so there are big differences within occupations between the status of women and men. For example, over 90% of medical, dental and veterinary workers are female, but only 33% of doctors, dentists and veterinarians are female. Women outnumber men in the finance, insurance and real estate sector of the economy, and constitute 61% of total staff in the banking industry (but they form 76% of the staff in the lowest three grades).

Although change is slow, an increasing proportion of those in senior positions are women. Since 1982, there has been a gradual increase in the number of women in senior teaching positions in primary and secondary schools, but major differences remain. In the banking industry in 1982 there were only three female bank managers out of 1,405 bank managers. A survey of six of the retail banks revealed 249 female managers out of 2,218 managers. In the public service, only 1% of workers at the top of the executive clerical grade or above were women in 1985; by 1988, this had risen to 7.6%.

A number of education and training programmes are aimed at increasing women's participation in non-traditional occupations and forms of recreation, and achieving better performance in all areas. These have been approved by the Human Rights Commission. Such programmes included women-only courses in carpentry, joinery, electronics, life skills, finance, business, science, engineering and assertiveness.

EQUAL PAY?

Paid employment is the main source of income for women aged under 60 in New Zealand. According to figures published by *Statistics New Zealand* in 1998, the average ordinary time weekly earnings for females was $552.99 and male's ordinary weekly pay was $707.46.

The positions of women and men in the distribution of market income are starkly and diametrically opposed. Women are concentrated in the lower income groups, men in the higher. In spite of this, the relative position of women has improved slightly, with a 3% increase in the proportion of women in the top two income groups, and a 3% decline in the number of men in these groups.

The reasons for the disparity in earnings are many, including women's lower labour force participation, their fewer average hours of paid work, greater likelihood of intermittent participation in paid work, and younger average age in the workforce, lower levels of education and different occupational distribution. A recent study suggests that these factors can explain at least two-thirds of gender differences in pay, leaving one-third unexplained.

Women of all ages are more likely than men to rely on income from welfare benefits and pensions. Benefits made up over 20% of the incomes of women under the age of 35 in 1988–89, compared with 5% of men's income in the same age group. For women aged 35–59, 14–15% of their income came from benefits compared with 2% of male income in the same period. Over the age of 60, 72% of women's incomes is derived from social welfare payments, compared with 49% it, of men's. Maori women are particularly dependent on welfare payments; benefits were the sole source of income for 47% of Maori women in 1981, compared to 25% of non-Maori women.

The Equal Pay Act 1972

The Equal Pay Act 1972 sought to remove discrimination in rates of remuneration based on the sex of employees. The Act has been interpreted as providing for equal pay rates for men and women doing the same work, although it does allow for special rates to be paid to employees on the basis of 'special qualities'. A difficulty lies in distinguishing whether payments are for special qualities or represent discrimination. The fact remains that women continue to earn significantly less than men.

While the pay gap between male and female earnings closed by seven percentage points (72% to 79%) between the passage of the Equal Pay Act 1972, and its final implementation in 1977, it has risen to only 81% in the past 15 years.

Despite the Equal Pay Act the distribution of market income is heavily weighted in favour of males as noted above. In all occupational groups male full-time employees receive higher median incomes than their female counterparts. This is so even in occupational groups which are predominantly female, such as clerical work. Even though 74% of clerical workers are female, they earn on average only 73% of the average male clerical worker's pay. In the service and sales occupation groups in 1986, men's full-time median incomes were respectively 73% and 69% higher than women's.

In the higher paid occupational groups the gaps are not quite as large. Male full-time managers and administrators have a median income which is 48% higher than their female co-workers, while for male professional and technical workers it is 39% higher. This is probably a reflection of the higher education qualifications which are required for these occupations, which attract some measure of higher reward. However, even where qualifications are equal, women do not earn as much as men. For example, in 1986 only 17% of women with tertiary qualifications earned over $20,000, compared to half all men with similar qualifications. Nearly half of all women with tertiary qualifications earned $10,000 or less compared with only 15% of men. A lack of qualifications has a significant impact on the incomes of Maori women, whose full-time earnings in 1986 were over $2,000 less than that of all women. Of this difference, 30% has been attributed to lack of qualifications.

Latest figures show average ordinary time weekly earnings for men of $628.34 in 1994, $667.84 in 1996 and $707.46 in 1998. In comparison women earned $484.85 in 1994, $512.87 in 1996 and $522.99 in 1998.

CURRENT ATTITUDES IN NEW ZEALAND

Thankfully the New Zealand male isn't as 'crass' as his Australian counterpart, who so often likes to refer to all women as 'Sheilas'. Perhaps this is an inordinate fondness for women named 'Sheila', or even a huge memory lapse!

The modern New Zealand male is more sensitive, and in many cases the male has taken over the traditional female role in bringing up the family whilst the woman pursues her career, or perhaps finishes her studies. There are, however, still pockets of males who continue to denigrate the female into the 'house help' role. Some New Zealand males still retain the 'settlers' mentality of hard living and hard drinking, rugby and racing.

The attitude of some men towards females, who compete for jobs in a male dominated workforce, especially in manual work areas, is that expressed by Arthur Daley of the TV series *Minder*, *ie* 'her indoors', or the well worn phrase 'the little woman at home'. We can only hope that such labelling of women will soon be a thing of the past. Here in New Zealand we are working towards that. Let's hope we are the first to achieve this, as we were with votes for women.

'Women Should Not Imitate Men'
A recent article in a Christchurch newspaper by General Eva Burrows of the Salvation Army said:

'In seeking equality, women should not imitate men. They must remember the feminine factor, they have their own psyche, gifts and talents. We can be equal but different. This world is very aggressive, competitive and masculine. It needs the feminine touch. You despoil your characteristics if you try to lead in a masculine way. Women should not be limited to a life in the home, it was right for them to take their place in all the professions.'

LIFE FOR RURAL WOMEN

According to the report *Status of New Zealand Women 1992*, rural women continue to form only a small percentage (14%) of the total female population. This includes women living in rural settlements as well as those living on farms. (The term 'rural' is defined as those areas outside centres of population of 1,000 or more people.)

New Zealand women have traditionally been well organised. For example the **Country Women's Institute** cements social bonds; the **Women's Division Federated Farmers** (WDFF) acts as a lobby group within Federated Farmers (the major association of New Zealand farmers) and between farming women and the rest of society; and since 1980 **Women in Agriculture** (WAG) has developed a support network for women moving into non-traditional roles and employment in agriculture.

What a rural survey showed

A 1989 survey by rural women's organisations showed that:

- Women who live on farms do 80% of the household duties.

- 60% of farms have only one unpaid worker (usually paid in kind with housing, food etc) and 70% have no paid employees.

- 80% of farm women work with the stock but most do not decide what will be done or how it will be done.

- Only 30% of farm women regard themselves as farmers. Almost half regard themselves primarily as homemakers, but are expected to assist on the farm as required at short notice, usually for no pay.

- 40% of farm women work in paid employment off the farm, and 30% believe that this is essential to supplement farm income. Women are more likely to work off the farm than men, but are constrained by a lack of job opportunities in rural areas. Some farm women have taken up paid work in towns and return to the farm only at weekends.

'For home and country'

The **Federation of Country Women's Institutes of New Zealand** has four aims: to unite women to promote the international motto – 'for home and for country'; to foster handicrafts, choral, drama, and other cultural activities; to encourage participation in community and national affairs; and to promote international understanding and goodwill through the organisation, **Associated Country Women of the World** (ACWW).

Women's Division Federation Farmers (WDFF) began life in 1925 with 16 members. A Mr L H McAlpine, an organiser for the Farmers Union, helped start this organisation. He had been shocked to learn of the conditions facing many rural women – primitive houses, bad roads, isolation, loneliness, illness and lack of help of any kind. The **Emergency Housekeeping Service** was established and still exists today, now known by another name, **Home Care**.

During the war years, as well as knitting socks and sending parcels to the troops, the WDFF raised 5,000 pounds sterling to buy a Spitfire aeroplane for the defence of Britain. This very large sum was raised in just one month from donations and the collection of scrap metal. In the 1950s an education bursary was established and since then there have been many grants and bursaries for rural people to take up education opportunities.

Today, the WDFF is concerned to establish a national rural health task force to monitor the impact of the health reforms in rural areas; promote rural equity issues on special education funding; and regenerate interests in neighbourhood support groups to fight increasing crime levels in country areas. They are also promoting the role of rural women in small business and tourism ventures to diversify their economic bases. Among other occasions in their celebrations of the women's suffrage centenary, WDFF is organising Project Tree – a nationwide kowhai tree planting scheme.

WOMEN'S SOCIAL OPPORTUNITIES

A survey done by the Hillary Commission for Recreation and Sport in 1990 showed that women do less vigorous physical activity than men. A total of 32% of males and 24% of females get the quality and quantity of exercise necessary for aerobic fitness, whereas over 40% of women and less than 40% of men do moderate physical activity. Most of the difference was due to doing housework, done by 93% of women but only 59% of men.

Until age 11, boys and girls were equally active, but male activity increased slightly after the age of 11 (by 2%) and female activity decreased (by 10%). There was a marked difference in girls' and boys' preferred physical activities: girls favoured dancing, horse-riding and netball, while boys preferred cricket, rugby union, skateboarding and soccer.

It was found that women were less likely to run or jog than men (27% female, 41% male) but more likely to swim (29% female, 26% male). Walking was equally popular with both sexes. Women were more likely to do fitness exercises at home or go to a fitness class, and were more likely than men to exercise alone.

The three most popular exercises for women were swimming, cycling and aerobics, and for men swimming, snooker/pool and cycling. Young men under 18 play rugby and tennis, and young women play tennis. Older men and women play golf and lawn bowls.

Clubs for women

There are many types of clubs for women, ranging from the Church groups, such as 'Young Wives'. I joined such a group when I first arrived, and met a good range of people, and still retain contact with them, even though I am no longer a 'young wife'. There are also professional clubs, for females only, and **Toastmasters** which is usually a male and female organisation. The best way to find out about the range of clubs available to you is to contact the Citizens Advice Bureau nearest to you, and they will give you a complete run down.

● Citizens Advice Bureau, 305 Queen Street, Auckland. Tel: 64-9-377 3314.

And don't forget the YWCA which is alive and well in all the main areas.

If you enjoy outdoor sports, there are always golf clubs to join. and outdoor bowls is another very popular sport. If you feel a little more energetic there are plenty of tennis clubs, squash clubs and swimming and also athletic clubs.

THE COST OF LOOKING GOOD

A visit to the hairdresser for a cut, shampoo and set costs in the region of $78–$98 for women and $58–$68 for men, depending upon the standard of hairdressing salon. To have highlights or a permanent colour with a set would cost up to $113, a tint would be $63, a semi permanent would start around $53 and a perm would cost around $98–$153.

Correct dress is advisable for a career woman, and a suit would cost in the region of $300–$600. Casual wear is the order of the day for holidays and weekends, and after work occasions, and there are lots of shops to tempt you. They range from the **Katies** shops, which are Australian, importing all the clothes from Australia at very reasonable prices, to the small boutiques, which are usually privately owned, and stock the more unusual lines of clothing, to the larger department stores like **Kirkaldie & Stains** in Wellington and **Smith & Caughey** in Auckland, where you can choose from a large range of clothes to suit all occasions. **Farmers** is a cheaper range department store with branches throughout New Zealand; there you can buy anything from a plant pot to a new coat.

If you live in the north of the North Island, you will find you can probably survive the 'winter' with a lightweight coat or raincoat. But if you live in the lower half of the North Island, or in the South Island, you will need a warm winter coat. This will typically cost somewhere between $200 and $500.

Shoes can cost between $100 and $200 for New Zealand made, to $150–$300 and even more for imported ones.

Perfume is quite expensive, due largely to the high import cost. A few price comparisons:

Estee Lauder

White Linen	100ml	$ 93
	50ml	$ 72
	25ml	$ 49
Oscar de la Renta	30ml	$ 80
Eau de Toilette	2fl. oz	$130
Opium	30ml	$ 89
Chanel Allure	30ml	$130

Makeup prices are as follows:
Revlon

Night cream	$ 50
Day cream	$ 40
Foundation	$ 35
Blusher	$ 30
Lipstick	$ 19.70

Estee Lauder

Cleanser	$ 50
Toner	$ 46

Night repair cream	$155
Moisturiser	$130
Makeup base	$ 72
Foundation cream	$ 70

These are just a few examples of the prices you can expect to pay in New Zealand. These are by no means the only cosmetics you can buy here, as all the cosmetic companies are selling very well in New Zealand.

SOME FAMOUS NEW ZEALAND WOMEN

Jean Batten
Born in Rotorua in 1909, died in Jamaica in 1982 of an untreated dog bite. Jean Batten was one of the world's pioneer women aviators, establishing a string of world records in the mid-1930s. Her tally as a record-holding solo pilot includes four world records for any type of plane, and another five important records. During the war she worked as an ambulance driver in France and in a munitions factory in Dorset, having failed the eye test for the Air Transport Auxiliary of the RAF.

Katherine Mansfield
Born in Wellington in 1888 and died in Fontainbleau in 1923. Katherine Mansfield is New Zealand's best known and respected author. Her work has earned her an international reputation as one of the finest short story writers in English. Her work has been translated into 20 languages.

Malvina Major
Born in Hamilton in 1943. She was awarded an OBE in 1985 and a DBE in 1991. Malvina Major has one of the finest lyric soprano voices in the world, particularly suited to the music of Rossini, Bellini, Donizetti and Mozart. She received wide acclaim for her international performance in Rossini's *Elizabetta Regina d'Ingliterra* at London's Camden Festival and in 1960 made her international debut at the Saltzburg Festival as Rosina in the *Barber of Seville*.

Kiri Te Kanawa
Born in Gisborne in 1944. She studied under Sister Mary Leo from 1959 to 1965. Kiri left New Zealand at the age of 21 to study at the

London Opera Centre. Upon graduating, Kiri joined the Royal Opera House, Covent Garden, making her debut in 1971 as Xenia in *Boris Godonov* by Moussorgsky. She is world renowned and especially remembered for singing at the wedding of Prince Charles and Lady Diana Spencer.

Kate Sheppard
Born in Liverpool in 1848, and died in 1934. Kate was a very able leader, and between 1888 and 1893 she organised five petitions to Parliament calling for women to be included as voters in general elections. Rejected one after the other, the petitions gained more signatures, until the fifth in 1893 carried the names of 31,872 women, about a third of the adult female population at that time. On 19 September 1893, as a result of determined campaigning, the Electoral Bill received the Governor's consent.

Yvette Williams
Born in Dunedin in 1929. Yvette jumped a record-breaking 6.24 metres in the long jump, making her the first New Zealand woman to win a gold medal at an Olympiad. She won four gold British Empire Games medals and set a world record for the long jump between 1950 and 1954. She has won many other events, and was named New Zealand Sportsman of the Year (an award won by a woman only once before) in both 1950 and 1952.

Annelise Coberger
Born in Christchurch in 1971. Her Bavarian grandfather, Oscar Coberger, had been his region's ski champion. He emigrated to New Zealand in 1926 and opened the country's first ski shop at Arthur's Pass. With such an illustrious parentage it is no wonder that Annelise was so keen on skiing. At 18 years she won the prestigious German junior slalom championships. In 1991 with an international ranking of fifth in the slalom event, she climbed from a world ranking of 86th to be placed 24th. In the 1991–92 northern winter she won her first World Cup.

Amy Block
New Zealand's most notorious woman was undoubtedly Amy Block, the confidence trickster. She spent her life fabricating a series of personalities and complicated scenarios in order to gain money. She spent nearly half her career in prison from 1884 to 1909. When

not in prison she obtained work as a cook or housekeeper defrauding her employers of money and possessions. She created a variety of personas, including Miss Crisp, Mrs Merry, Mrs Chanel and Charlotte Skevington. Her greatest coup was in 1908 when she posed as Percy Carol Redwood, passing herself off as a wealthy young man (the nephew of a Bishop!); while taking a holiday in Port Molyneaux, she courted a landlady's daughter. They married with 200 guests attending the wedding. Her fraudulent behaviour was her undoing, and she was put on trial for false pretences in 1909.

QUESTIONS AND ANSWERS

How many women in New Zealand own farms?

Fewer than five per cent of farms are owned by women with sole titles. Most of these come through inheritance as a widow or daughter, rather than by independent purchase.

What pre-school care is there for children?

Kindergartens and playcentres are very popular in all areas. Full-time kindergarten care for the working mother would cost around $100 per week.

10

Leisure Opportunities

In 1998, 1,457,000 people travelled to New Zealand to holiday or visit family and friends.

AROUND AND ABOUT THE NORTH ISLAND

The Bay of Islands

Starting in the 'winterless north' there are so many beautiful beaches you would find it hard to choose which was the best. The **Bay of Islands**, with Paihia the most popular holiday resort, is the most beautiful holiday spot. From here you can go on the 'Fullers Cream Trip' on a modern catamaran – *The Big Cat* – and cruise around all the beautiful little coves in luxury, dropping off at Russell, an old settlement across the harbour from Paihia. There are lots of game fishing launches which can be privately hired, or you can just pay to go on a trip on one and catch the 'big one'.

Accommodation is covered in this area by bed and breakfast, motels, hotels, luxury lodges and resorts. For comprehensive and up-to-date information on location and prices for these accommodation options go to *www.purenz.com*. Information can also be obtained from New Zealand Tourism Offices overseas.

The Coromandel Peninsula

Travelling south through Auckland, the next notable holiday favourite with New Zealanders is the **Coromandel Peninsula**. Here you will find many beautiful secluded shores, with bush and grass verging onto the beaches. At Hahei Beach, named after a legendary Maori explorer, you will find two Maori Pa sites at the southern end, and beyond that two 'blowholes' which can provide a spectacular sight at high tide. A two hour return walk at the northern end of the beach leads to a large sea-formed cavern known as Cathedral Cave.

Accommodation is covered in this area by bed and breakfast, motels, hotels, luxury lodges, resorts and holiday homes. For comprehensive and up-to-date information on location and prices for these accommodation options go to *www.purenz.com*. Information can also be obtained from New Zealand Tourism Offices overseas.

The Bay of Plenty
South once more, we reach the **Bay of Plenty**, renowned for its wonderful long expanse of white sands. Mount Maunganui is the most popular holiday spot, especially for the young people, who find lots to do during their summer holidays, from bungy-jumping to white water rafting. This is the place to go if you are looking for a hectic New Year's Eve, with bands and open air concerts all the rage. Tauranga, the main city of the Bay of Plenty, lies across the harbour from Mount Maunganui. There is a harbour bridge for easy access. Here you will find an excellent selection of shops and facilities. A big feature of this area is the Hot Water Sea Pool complex at Mount Maunganui. Here you can luxuriate in wonderful temperatures all year round. There is nothing nicer on a cold miserable day than to go along to the Pools. To lie in the lovely hot water at night to look at the stars is a great experience.

Accommodation is covered in this area by bed and breakfast, motels, hotels, luxury lodges, resorts, holiday homes and homestays. For comprehensive and up-to-date information on location and prices for these accommodation options go to *www.purenz.com*. Information can also be obtained from New Zealand Tourism Offices overseas.

The Lakes
Inland now to the Lakes, to Lake Rotorua first. Here you will be able to sightsee to your heart's content, as this is the place to be for the traditional Maori Concert Parties, and Maori Hangi's, the Maori way of cooking. A hole is dug in the ground, lined with stones, and a fire lit. The stones heat up, and when they are hot enough, food wrapped in sacks is lowered into the pit. These are then covered and the food left to cook for many hours. The results are delicious. Rotorua is a land of thermal activity with hot water geysers and hot mud pools – many of the motels in this area have their own thermally heated spa pools. The imposing Tudor Towers, set amongst beautiful gardens, is the place where the early settlers used to flock to 'take the waters' with a bathhouse built for rheumatic people. The fishing is excellent here, the lakes and streams abounding with big fish. At the Rainbow Springs visitors

centre you can feed large trout by hand in the pools which run through this area – no fishing is allowed here though!

Accommodation is covered in this area by bed and breakfast, motels, hotels, luxury lodges, resorts, holiday homes, homestays and backpackers. For comprehensive and up-to-date information on location and prices for these accommodation options go to *www.purenz.com*. Information can also be obtained from New Zealand Tourism Offices overseas.

Lake Taupo

Lake Taupo lies in the centre of New Zealand's central volcanic plateau. Here is the world famous Wairakei geothermal hydro-electric power establishment. Lake Taupo itself is a very popular retreat for many a 'top person' or movie star wanting a peaceful fishing holiday. This is where you always catch 'the big one'! Here also are thermal hot baths, the AC Baths being a very popular venue. There is also an old historic hotel, De Bretts Thermal Resort, with two large thermal mineral outdoor pools, freshwater pools and 12 private minerals pools. Here the early settlers used to come to soak their rheumatic limbs in the comforting waters.

Taupo also makes a good stopping off point for the ski fields just 90km south, at Tongariro National Park.

If you are a golfing fan, you can play a round on the internationally famous Wairakei Golf Course, or maybe the Taupo Golf Course further into town would suit you. Lake Taupo itself offers a variety of attractions with yachting, water skiing, jet boating and rowing.

Accommodation is covered in this area by bed and breakfast, motels, hotels, luxury lodges, resorts, holiday parks, and homestays. For comprehensive and up-to-date information on location and prices for these accommodation options go to *www.purenz.com*. Information can also be obtained from New Zealand Tourism Offices overseas.

Mount Egmont

We can cross now to the west coast and New Plymouth, with Mount Egmont National Park on the doorstep, an ideal environment for the tramper, or we can take it easy and use the Mount Egmont daily shuttles.

Golfers have a choice of nine golf courses; bowlers are very welcome in all the clubs; and fishing enthusiasts will be well satisfied with the rivers and streams.

Accommodation is covered in this area by bed and breakfast, motels, hotels, luxury lodges, resorts, holiday parks, homestays and backpackers. For comprehensive and up-to-date information on location and prices for these accommodation options go to *www.purenz.com*. Information can also be obtained from New Zealand Tourism Offices overseas.

Sightseeing in Wellington
South to the capital Wellington, where there is sightseeing in abundance: you can either go around at your own pace, or join one of the city tours – either of these is certainly a 'must' to explore the steep hills, narrow crowded streets, Parliament, a quaint cable car, art galleries, a zoo and the Botanic Gardens to mention a few.

Accommodation is covered in this area by bed and breakfast, motels, hotels, serviced apartments and backpackers. For comprehensive and up-to-date information on location and prices for these accommodation options go to *www.purenz.com*. Information can also be obtained from New Zealand Tourism Offices overseas.

DISCOVERING THE SOUTH ISLAND

From Wellington you can cross to the South Island by sea or air. By sea you can cross with your car at around $190 for the car each way, $59 per adult $35 per child each way. The alternative is to cross by sea at a cost of $59 and catch the Mount Cook Landline Coach to your destination. The coach will meet the ferry and take you to Christchurch for $132 per person. To fly across to, say, Christchurch from Wellington will cost around $250 one way by Air New Zealand or Ansett.

In the South Island the scenery is equal to anywhere in Switzerland, with the majestic mountains begging you to go skiing (in the winter of course!).

Picton
Why not stop awhile in Picton, where you will alight from the ferry? Picton is the principal centre of Marlborough Sounds, a breathtakingly beautiful scenic reserve with regular launch cruises in and around the bays in Queen Charlotte Sound. You can also take a fishing trip and a moonlight cruise during the summer months.

Accommodation is covered in this area by bed and breakfast, motels, hotels, luxury lodges, resorts, holiday parks, homestays and backpackers. For comprehensive and up-to-date information on location and prices for these accommodation options go to *www.purenz.com*. Information can also be obtained from New Zealand Tourism Offices overseas.

Christchurch

Christchurch has a lot to offer, with lovely parks and reserves, and the Avon River idling through gives a peaceful restful feeling – even though Christchurch itself is a very busy tourism centre. You can make your base here whilst you visit all the places of interest, as Christchurch is fairly central, and has excellent transport facilities.

Accommodation is covered in this area by bed and breakfast, motels, hotels, luxury lodges, resorts, holiday parks, homestays and backpackers. For comprehensive and up-to-date information on location and prices for these accommodation options go to *www.purenz.com*. Information can also be obtained from New Zealand Tourism Offices overseas.

Queenstown

Queenstown is a must, even out of the ski season. There is windsurfing, water skiing and fishing to be had – not forgetting the excitement of white water raft trips and exhilarating jet boat rides on the nearby rivers. Ride on horseback along the original goldmining trail to the historic town of Moonlight, or by mini-coach to the beautiful Skippers Canyon, also steeped in goldmining history. For the more leisurely minded, a trip on the *SS Earnslaw* on Lake Wakatipu is a delight. The scenery is wonderful.

Accommodation is covered in this area by bed and breakfast, motels, hotels, luxury lodges, resorts, holiday parks, homestays and backpackers. For comprehensive and up-to-date information on location and prices for these accommodation options go to *www.purenz.com*. Information can also be obtained from New Zealand Tourism Offices overseas.

Franz Josef

Up the west coast of the South Island you will pass through Haast Pass, Fox Glacier and then onto Franz Josef. This is a small tourist centre near the northern boundary of Westland National Park. Franz Josef is a tranquil settlement nestled amongst the splendid native forest of the coast under the massive peaks of the Southern Alps. There are many safe, pleasant walking tracks in the surrounding bush and foothills of the mountains. Of particular interest is the Franz Josef Glacier, which is a short walk or drive from the town.

Accommodation is covered in this area by bed and breakfast, motels, hotels, holiday parks and backpackers. For comprehensive and up-to-date information on location and prices for these accommodation options go to *www.purenz.com*. Information can also be obtained from New Zealand Tourism Offices overseas.

Nelson

Moving on northwards still, passing through Hokitika, Greymouth until you reach Nelson. Nelson has the reputation of being one of the sunniest spots in New Zealand. It is sheltered by the hills, and has fine mountain, river and lake scenery. There are golden beaches – Tahuna, Rabbit Island and Cable Bay. At Tahuna there is a children's playground, skating rink and golf course.

Accommodation is covered in this area by bed and breakfast, motels, hotels, luxury lodges, resorts, holiday parks, homestays and backpackers. For comprehensive and up-to-date information on location and prices for these accommodation options go to *www.purenz.com*. Information can also be obtained from New Zealand Tourism Offices overseas.

SKIING IN NEW ZEALAND

The skiing season in New Zealand extends from June to late October at ski areas in the North and South Islands. Many fields also have snow-making equipment to ensure reliable snow depth and quality. New Zealand has 12 commercial ski areas, 12 club ski fields and one commercial cross-country ski area.

In the North Island the main skiing centre is Mount Ruapehu in the Tongariro National Park. There are two commercial ski fields, Whakapapa and Turoa, and one club field (Tukino) at Ruapehu, with the Manuganui ski club area in Mount Egmont in Taranaki (New Plymouth).

In the South Island the commercial ski areas are Coronet Peak, the Remarkables (Queenstown), Cardrona, Treble Cone (Wanaka) Ohau, Mount Dobson (Aorangi), Porter Heights, Mount Hutt, Mount Lyford (Canterbury), and Rainbow Valley (Marlborough). There are ten smaller ski club fields in the South Island.

The Waioru Nordic Ski Area on the Pisa Range near Wanaka offers 24 kilometres of cross-country skiing. Glacier skiing on the

Tasman and Fox Glaciers, with access via ski-planes, is also available, while guided heliskiing and ski touring open up the Ben Ohau Ranges, the Harris Mountains, the Two Thumbs Range, the Mount Cook/Tasman Glacier area, Mount Hutt and Queenstown in the South island and the Ruahine Ranges in the North.

Winter skiing holiday packages

There are a variety of package holiday specialists that are listed on the website for Tourism New Zealand at *www.purenz.com*. Skiing is such a large part of the New Zealand winter that these companies can cater to your specific needs and at your level of budget. Whether you want to go skiing, snowboarding or heliskiing on one mountain or many they will provide you with a package deal to suit you. Both Air New Zealand and Ansett offer competitive deals in the winter season but these prices vary seasonally. So the best idea if planning a skiing holiday in New Zealand is to go to the Tourism New Zealand site and have a look at the package deals on offer and also check your local papers for hot deals. Information can be obtained and your holiday booked from New Zealand Tourism Offices overseas.

Transportation

By bus

There are two main bus passenger operators that provide daily scheduled services through the country. **Newmans Coach Line** provide services in the North Island and around the major tourist routes in the South Island, while **Intercity Coachlines** operate the largest network throughout both islands.

Travelling by coach is an easy way to see New Zealand in comfort. All accommodation, meals and baggage are taken care of and the driver or guide often provides a commentary, pointing out all the significant sites and stories relating to historic events or Maori legend. Most destinations have several departures daily. You can book in advance but this is not usually necessary.

Newmans Coach Lines have timetables for both the North and South Island. They offer a **Stopover Pass**, which means that you can travel for up to three months over a selected route travelling whenever and wherever you want. The North Island pass takes you from Auckland to Wellington via the main cities for around $95 for adults. The South Island pass travels from Christchurch to Queenstown via Milford Sound for around $132 for adults. For more information about this service contact Newmans Coach Lines on Tel: 64-9-913 6121. Fax: 64-9-913 6200.

Intercity Coachlines have three different comprehensive packages: a **North Island pass**, a **South Island pass** and a **New Zealand pass**, and within each pass there is a variety of different travel routes to cater to your plans, giving total flexibility as to when and where you want to go. For more information contact Intercity Coachlines on Tel: 64-9-913 6121. Fax: 64-9-913 6200. E-mail: *info@coachnet.co.nz*.

Renting a car
Discover New Zealand for yourself. All international car rental businesses are available in every major city. Budget, Hertz, Avis as well as a few local companies offer comprehensive motoring on New Zealand's uncongested, good quality roads.

Rent-a-Dent has branches all through New Zealand. They supply quality rental vehicles and competitive prices. They have cars, station wagons and campervans for hire. Cars start from $59 per day and a mini coach from $95 per day. These prices include unlimited kilometres, and GST (Goods and Services Tax of 12.5%), but not insurance. For further information contact the Auckland branch at 105 Cook Street. Tel: 64-9-309 0066. Website: *www.rentadent.co.nz*.

Two-wheel rentals
You can also tour New Zealand on two wheels. Mike Vinsen, a licensed motor vehicle dealer at 300 Great North Road, Grey Lynn, Auckland, Tel: 64-9-827, has 6,619 motorcycles, mopeds and scooters for rental, with helmets and riding gear also available.

BACKPACKING AND FARM HOLIDAYS

Backpacking
Backpacking is a very popular form of holidaying. There are hostels in most tourist towns and cities, where you would expect to pay an average of $20 per night for single accommodation, $15 for shared. These prices include Goods and Services Tax. All hostels have self cook kitchens, laundry facilities and common areas where you can meet and exchange information with fellow travellers. You do not have to be a member to stay at any of the hostels, and no institutional rules apply. Linen and blankets are available for hire, though some hostels supply these free.

Discount cards
Discounts have been arranged for many backpackers' hotels, from

film developing and tandem parapenting, to cheap fruit and vegetables. Many hostels have VIP cards so you can take advantage of these discounts.

Some discount cards give excellent travel discounts – 50% off Air New Zealand and Ansett New Zealand domestic fares, 30% off Intercity Coaches and Trains, 10% off Kiwi Experience-Backpackers Adventure Travel, and 10% off Fiordland Travel (South Island). These specials are available on the **VIP Backpackers Discount Card** which can be purchased for $20 and is valid for 12 months. For further information write to: Back Packers Accommodation Council of New Zealand, level 15, Price Water House, corner of Hobson and Wyndham Streets, Auckland, New Zealand. Tel: 64-9-377 4714.

Farms and homestays

Farms and homestays are a popular way of spending a holiday. What better way to get to know the New Zealanders than by staying in their homes with them as a host or hostess? Tourism New Zealand has 59 farmstays listings. To view these go to their website at: *www.purenz.com.*

It may be the perfect opportunity to get away from city life and take a walk in the clean country air or you may want to join in with the farm's day-to-day running or you may like to try a traditional New Zealand home cooked meal. Many farmstays are close to an abundance of outdoor activities like skiing, horse riding, and fishing. Homestay accommodation tends to find something to suit everyone.

Farm homestays mean living on a typical working farm, varying in size from 100 to over 10,000 acres, often running upwards of several thousand sheep. In addition you can find dairy farms, orchards and properties with horticulture.

Country homestays are usually based on a few acres in the country, handy to a major city or town. They usually run some sheep, and possibly other animals such as deer and goats. Quite often country home hosts are retired farmers, or they may work in a nearby town or city. These are referred to as 'lifestyle blocks'.

To get a run down on prices for homestays go to *www.purenz.com* and contact the places of your choice through their internet sites or phone numbers.

It is advisable to book your farm or homestay as far in advance as possible to secure the properties of your choice, especially from November through to February. A holiday can also be booked through your local travel agent. Bookings and information can also be obtained from New Zealand Tourism Offices overseas.

YOUTH HOSTELLING

Youth hostelling is a very popular way to see New Zealand. For information contact New Zealand Youth Hostel Association, Auckland. Tel: 64-9-309 2802. Fax: 64-9-303 9525.

The traveller must be aware of the fact that New Zealand is no longer free of crime, and you must always keep in mind the following:

- Do not travel alone.
- Do not hitch hike.
- Do not give lifts to strangers.
- Do not leave valuables in cars.
- Do not place yourself in an isolated situation.
- Always be aware of dangerous situations just as you would at home, and in the rest of the world.
- Do not place your trust in a smiling face.

VISITING NEW ZEALAND'S ISLAND NEIGHBOURS

The beauty of living here in the Pacific Ocean is the number of idyllic islands available for the holiday of a lifetime. If you dream of two weeks basking in the sun on a 'Robinson Crusoe' type island, then you will be able to take your pick.

Vanuatu (formerly the New Hebrides)

This is a chain of more than 80 islands, only three hours' flying time from Auckland. This diverse country's features include active volcanoes, coral islands and wide sandy bays with luxuriant tropical vegetation. The time zone is one hour behind New Zealand.

The population are Melanesian inhabitants born in Vanuatu and called ni-Vanuatu. The country's population is about 130,000. The official languages are English, French and Bislama (pidgin English). Summer is from November to March with an average of 28 degrees Celsius and winter from April to October with an average temperature of 23 degrees Celsius. Dress is casual, but not *too* brief: tropical clothes for men's evening wear and light dresses or skirts for ladies. The cost of a seven day stay is around $939 per person to $2,000 per person.

Fiji

Fiji is 300 islands of beaches, reefs, corals, forests, rivers and peace! If you are a lover of *Treasure Island, Robinson Crusoe* or *Mutiny on the Bounty* this is the place to be! Here you can see the water though which Captain Bligh sailed after the mutiny; you can picnic on deserted islands, see old cannibal ovens, and let fish nibble your toes.

Fiji has something for everyone, with accommodation from extreme luxury to affordable budget. It is a paradise for back-packers, not only because of the wide range of affordable budget accommodation ranging from $5 upwards, but also because of the friendliness and genuine hospitality of the people. Seven days here will cost between $950 and $2,200 per person, depending on the time of year.

Norfolk Island

An interesting aspect of Norfolk Island is its colourful past filled with some of history's more notable seamen, such as Captain James Cook and the *Bounty* mutineers. From its early days as a convict settlement, the island has become an historian's paradise with its old buildings as from the penal days to the early homes of the Pitcairn settlers (*Bounty* descendants).

There is something to do all the time here, without repeating yourself too often – bush walks, snorkelling, fishing, surfing, diving, horse riding, gun clubs, golf, tennis or bowling, just to mention a few. There is a wide range of accommodation available, and seven days here would start from $1,100 per person.

Tonga

The kingdom of Tonga is an archipelago of some 170 islands scattered across the South Pacific near the International Date Line and just north of the tropic of Capricorn. Tonga remains a kingdom, its government a constitutional monarchy, and member of the British Commonwealth. The Head of State is King Taufa'ahau Tupou IV, son of the late Queen Salote. The capital is Nuku'alofa.

It is claimed that Tonga has been inhabited since 500BC and Tongans are descended from 'Lapita' people, the forerunners of today's Polynesians. The climate is cooler and less humid than most tropical areas. The average daily temperature is 24 degrees Celsius The hottest months are December/January. Seven days here will cost approximately $800 to $1,600 per person. There is a wide range of accommodation.

The Cook Islands

One of the best things about Rarotonga and the Cook Islands as a holiday destination is that it can be whatever you want to make it: sunshine, crystal clear lagoon waters, with swimming, sailing, windsurfing, scuba diving, tennis, golf, bowls, squash, canoeing and many more activities. Accommodation is varied with both budget and luxury hotels, the approximate cost for seven days being $1,300 to $2,600 per person.

THE GREAT OUTDOORS

New Zealand recreation is generally aimed at the great outdoors! The obvious beach activities include swimming. snorkelling and year round activities such as wind surfing and sailing.

Sport, fitness and leisure have played a key part in creating and shaping New Zealand's national image, both at home and abroad, and contribute much to the lifestyle New Zealanders enjoy. Everyone has the chance to take part in some form of sport or leisure activity and it is government policy to promote access to it for all New Zealanders.

An extensive and varied park system which includes national, forest and maritime parks, historic and scenic reserves, walkways and many local parks and reserves, showcases the environment and provides a full spectrum of recreational opportunity.

Top sports for people over the age of 15 years are swimming/ diving, cycling, snooker/pool, tennis and aerobics. In the recreational physical activity section walking comes out tops followed by running/jogging, cycling and fitness classes. In terms of favourite leisure activities reading is the most popular followed by watching television and videos, visiting friends, listening to music and gardening.

Marching is a New Zealand-born sport, originating in the early years of the 1930s Depression. The grades in marching cover four age groups, the senior grade for those 16 years and over, the junior grade for girls aged 12 to 16, the midget grade for seven to 12 year olds, and the introductory grade for six to 12 year olds.

There is a large following for big game fishing, lake and river fishing. Shooting and hunting is very popular, the principal game birds being duck, swan, pheasant, quail, geese and chukor. The season is, however, limited to six to eight weeks starting on the first weekend of May.

Skiing, mountaineering, tramping and walking offer an immense variety of venues to people in all age groups.

Golfing and bowls (indoor and outdoor) are also very popular, with a huge selection of clubs throughout New Zealand.

For the more daring, there is white water rafting, abseiling, mountain climbing, parachuting, gliding and bungy-jumping. You can find these and a lot more thrilling outdoor sports with up-to-date pricing on the Tourism New Zealand site *www.purenz.com*. Information can also be obtained from New Zealand Tourism Offices overseas.

DINING OUT

Over the past few years café style eating has become very popular. You will find tables to sit at outside cafés in most cities in New Zealand. Magazines and newspapers are available for you to read and an array of food and beverages from all-day breakfasts to vegan and vegetarian meals are on the menu.

Every style of restaurant and eating establishment is to be found now in most parts of New Zealand, with Thai, Italian, Spanish, Hungarian, Japanese, Chinese, New Zealand and European cuisines. You can expect to pay $20 to $30 for a fairly inexpensive meal, and for the high class establishments in top hotels and some of the more 'intimate' restaurants, somewhere in the region of $50 to $70 a head.

BYO – visitors will notice that many restaurants hold a 'byo' licence, that is, these establishments are permitted by law to allow clients to 'bring your own' liquor with them, to be consumed with their meal. There is usually a 'corkage' charge of $1–$3. Restaurants of this nature are distinct from those who are licensed to sell liquor on their premises.

A new feature of dining out which is becoming quite popular is the 'dessert' restaurants like 'Death by Chocolate' and 'Strawberry Faire'. Here you choose a dessert and finish up with coffee.

11

A Final Word

SOME TOPICAL ISSUES IN NEW ZEALAND

There are several topical issues concerning the New Zealand public, and you are likely to find them widely discussed. These are some of them.

Hardcore unemployment

People are becoming quite concerned at the growing number of redundancies, and the fact that so many people in the middle years are unable to find another job. The Government is now trying to encourage children to stay on at school, rather than leave and go 'on the dole': even after going to university and graduating, many young people are still unable to find work. There is also concern that there will be a core of people who will never be able to find employment in their lifetime again.

Health and education reforms

The Government has reorganised the health services, within the Ministry of Health, and people are worried when they see wards and hospitals closing down in the smaller areas. The Ministry of Health is leading the process of changes in the health sector and overviews the local and area Health Boards – they are working to make health services and hospitals become commercially viable organisations, rather than just a 'service'.

Schools have also been organised to run themselves, instead of the Education Department being responsible. School heads have been increasingly turned into administrators and schools are run by boards of trustees, elected from among the parents. The boards hire and fire, and because they have a strict budget to operate must hire to fit their budget; if they are short of money, they may feel obliged to hire less qualified teachers.

Crime
There is concern at the growing number of rapes, attacks of violence, murder and robbery. It is generally felt by the public that the punishment does not fit the crime. Offenders may be sentenced to eight to ten years, but this can be substantially reduced for good conduct. Also, white collar crime has increased, and seemingly 'stable' organisations have collapsed overnight when misappropriation of funds has been discovered. The prison population seems to be growing out of control.

Racism
Of concern to a lot of people is the Government's handling of the Treaty of Waitangi Appeals, and its 'hand-outs' to the Maori tribes. People in general feel that the other races in New Zealand are being disadvantaged because of this and instead of New Zealanders being 'one people' they are now split into 'them' and 'us'.

Many New Zealanders question the advisability of the Government's policy which allows large immigration of Asians. Some people are now shouting out against the seemingly 'over-run' situation. Asians are becoming prime targets for criminal elements.

A beautiful country
When Captain James Cook came ashore on the east coast in the late 1700s, he named the area the Bay of Plenty, and this it certainly is. Everything grows here aplenty. Grapefruit, orange and lemon trees are everywhere, dropping their fruit over lawns, road sides and fields.

Throughout New Zealand things grow in abundance. In the North Island you will see freesias growing wild at the roadside, arum lilies growing in fields, clematis growing amongst the trees in forest areas. In our garden in Tauranga in the Bay of Plenty, we grew outdoor tomatoes; the vines grew as abundantly as weeds, and black and green grapes were everywhere. There were plum trees, peach trees, guava trees, lemon and orange trees, to name but a few.

The commercialism so evident in most countries is still not alarmingly evident here. You will certainly not find the equivalent of Blackpool and the 'Golden Mile'. New Zealand has no really 'old' buildings, as it has only just been weaned in a historical sense. You will find several historic villages, where time seems to have stood still since the arrival of the early settlers; these are really a 'must' to view.

You will never grow bored with the scenery which changes

continually as you travel. The South Island is very grand with mountains to rival Switzerland. The peace you will feel because of the low population density is very captivating and you will feel very well rested after a holiday here.

Nuclear testing
In June 1995 the French Government announced the resumption of nuclear underground testing at Mururoa Atoll. This is a Pacific Island approximately 1,200km west of New Zealand. The people of New Zealand and other countries around the Pacific are very displeased with the arrogance of the French wanting to pollute our 'back garden'. The new Greenpeace *Rainbow Warrior* continues to police the environment of the southern hemisphere.

Gambling is alive and well in New Zealand
Many people live in the obscure hope that they will win a large fortune and retire into the lap of luxury. It is now more than a dream. New Zealand has extended the hand of opportunity to many by opening a casino in the South Island in Christchurch. My husband and I visited the casino in May 1995, and were amazed at the sight of people sitting patiently feeding 20c coins into the jaws of voracious slot machines lined up on two floors. Across the road from the casino was a prosperous pawnbroker, with many large diamond rings in his window, and next door a business that hired out appropriate clothes to punters to gain entry into the casino. Obviously the idea that 'one could lose one's pants at the races' could apply to the casino too. Auckland opened its magnificent casino in 1996 and one is planned for the waterfront in Wellington.

Black Magic!
The success of the New Zealand team in the Americas Yachting Cup in January 2000 was widely celebrated. Tickertape parades brought all the main New Zealand cities to a complete standstill. With the challenge returning to Auckland's shores again in 2002 the land close to the coast and around the viaduct area is being promoted by entrepreneurial real estate agents.

HOT OFF THE PRESS
- The health system is once again being restructured. As in the United Kingdom patients are being denied vital operations due

to quotas being imposed upon Health Authorities by government funding.

- The police are undermanned – computers are being put in offices rather than constables on the beat.

- Violent crime is on the increase and education standards are dropping.

- The Maori voice is being heard more, especially in Parliament with New Zealand now having the first Maori Deputy Prime Minister.

- The legal change of drinking regulations has occurred with the official lowering of the age limit to 18 years.

New plan to curb flood of migrants

The New Zealand Government is constantly looking for ways to slow the flood of new immigrants. This is reflected in the ever changing immigration requirements. It is very important to check with your nearest immigration department for the latest information.

POSTSCRIPT

Once you have discovered what a great place New Zealand is, you will need to give some serious thought to making the big move to live here, or whether you will just come for the holiday of a lifetime.

As far as my family and I are concerned, New Zealand has become our true home. My daughters have both graduated at university, and remember very little about England.

My husband and I are enjoying a type of semi-retirement, playing a little golf and writing books. We hope in the future to include lots of travel in our itinerary.

Don't be a 'nearly did'. Many people in England, upon hearing of our intentions to settle in New Zealand, said 'Oh, I nearly did that, but . . .' I decided there and then that I was never going to be a 'nearly did'. Life can be exciting if you give it a chance.

Good luck!

A Guide to Speaking New Zildish

One feature of New Zealand speech often commented on by visitors is the inordinate fondness for abbreviations which end in ie or y.

We put our cardies on when it's cold, our gummies when its muddy, our pinnies when cooking, our cossies when we go swimming, our nighties when going to bed.

Our buildings are usually erected by chippies, our boats are unloaded by wharfies, our mail delivered by posties. We buy food at the deli, send children to kindy and sometimes give a small donation to the Sallies. We fight for the best possie in front of the telly, to watch the footie. If it's an important match against the pommies we pull a sickie and take the day off work.

In summer we buy aerosols to spray the mozzies and blowies. We eat bickies and smoke ciggies. Some of us have been known to pull swifties and throw wobblies. Military types belong to the Terries. If the weather isn't iffy we have a barbie, and most of us have been to Aussie.

New Zildish translations

sickie	a day off work
togs & cossies	swimming costumes
barbie	barbecue
snarlers	sausages
Sallies	Salvation Army
possie	position
gummies	gum boots (wellingtons)
footie	football
chippies	builders
kindy	kindergarten
mozzies	mosquitoes
wobblies	tantrums
smoko	tea break time
chooks	chickens
this arvo	this afternoon

Pakeha	the Maori name for a European
she'll be right	everything will be fine
cobber	friend
mate	a quick name when you have forgotten!
your shout	your turn to buy drinks
chick	woman
Terries	Territorial Army
ciggies	cigarettes
Aussie	an Australian
Pom or Pommie	Englishman
the loo or dunny	the toilet
kick in the guts	give it all you have got
rough as guts	crude, unrefined, impolite
as full as a boot	drunk
surfie	surf board rider
nuddie	in the nude
wrinklies	old people
lollies	sweets, candy
dairy	the corner shop, sells a bit of everything, usually open seven days per week
to be sucked in	to be tricked into believing a lie

Useful Addresses

GENERAL INFORMATION ABOUT NEW ZEALAND

Christchurch Information Centre, corner of Worcester Boulevard and Oxford Terrace, Christchurch. Tel: 03 379 9629. Fax: 03 377 2424.

Hamilton Visitor Information Centre, Angelsea Street, Hamilton. Tel: 07 839 3580.

New Plymouth Public Relations & Marketing Office, Private Bag 2025, New Plymouth. Tel: 06 759 6086. Fax: 06 759 6073. E-mail: *info@newplymouth.govt.nz*.

North Shore Visitor Information Centre, 49 Hurstmere Road, Takapuna, Auckland. Tel: 09 486 8670.

Wellington Visitor Information Centre, 101 Wakefield Street, Wellington. Tel: 04 802 4860.

Newspapers UK

Destination New Zealand, Outbound Publishing, 1 Commercial Road, Eastbourne, East Sussex BN21 3QX. Tel: (01323) 726040.

New Zealand News UK, 25 Royal Opera Arcade, London SW1Y 4UY. Tel: (020) 7930 6451.

New Zealand Press Association, 12 Norwich Street, London EC4. Tel: (020) 7353 5430.

New Zealand Outlook, Consyl Publishing Ltd. 3 Bruckhurst Road, Bexhill-on-Sea TN40 1QF. Tel: (01424) 223111. Fax: (01424) 224992. Monthly newspaper.

TRAVEL (UK)

New Zealand High Commission Tourism Office, 80 Haymarket, London SW1Y 4TQ. Tel: 0839 300 900. Fax: (020) 7839 8929.

New Zealand Travel Information Service, 225 Riverside Gardens, London W6. Tel: (020) 8748 4455.

IMMIGRATION OFFICES

New Zealand Consulate General, Springsiedelgasse 28, A-1190 Wien, AUSTRIA. Tel: (1) 318 8505. Fax: (1) 377 660.

New Zealand Embassy, Boulevard du Regent 47-48, 1000 Brussels, BELGIUM. Tel: (2) 512 1040. Fax: (2) 513 4856. E-mail: *nzembbru@.compuserve.com*.

New Zealand High Commission, Suite 727, Metropolitan House, 99 Bank Street, Ottawa, Ontario K1P 6G3, CANADA. Tel: (613) 238 5991. Immigration: (613) 238 6097. Fax: (613) 238 5707. E-mail: *nzhcott@istar.com*.

New Zealand Consulate General, Suite 1200-888 Dunsmuir Street, PO Box 10-071, Pacific Centre, Vancouver, British Colombia V6C 3K4, CANADA. Tel: (604) 684 7388. Fax: (604) 684 7333.

New Zealand Embassy, 7 ter, Leonard de Vinci, 75116 Paris, FRANCE. Tel: (1) 4500 2411. Fax: (1) 4501 2639. E-mail: *nzembassv.paris@wanadoo.fr*.

New Zealand Immigration Service, Atrium Friedrichstrasse 60, 10117 Berlin, GERMANY. Tel: (30) 206 210. Fax: (30) 206 21114.

New Zealand Consulate General, Heimhuderstrasse 56, 20148 Hamburg, GERMANY. Tel: (40) 442 5550. Fax: (40) 425 5549.

New Zealand Consulate General, c/o Coopers & Lybrand, 24 Xenias Street, Athens 115 28, GREECE. Tel: (1) 771 0112. Fax: (1) 777 7390.

New Zealand Consulate General, 6501 General Plaza, 18 Harbour Road, Wanchai, HONG KONG, SAR China. Tel: 2525 5044. Immigration: 2877 4488. Fax: 2845 2915. Immigration: 2877 0586.

New Zealand Consulate General, 46 Upper Mount Street, Dublin 2, IRELAND. Tel: (01) 676 2464. Fax: (01) 676 2489.

New Zealand Embassy, Via Zara 28, Rome 00198, ITALY. Tel: (06) 441 7171. Fax: (06) 440 2984. E-mail: *nzemb.rom@flashnet.it*.

New Zealand Consulate, Villa Hampstead, Oliver Agius Street, Attard BZNO3 MALTA. Tel: (435) 025. Fax: (437) 200.

New Zealand Embassy, Embajada de Nueva Zelandia, Jose Luis Lagrange 103, 10th Floor, Colonia Los Morales, Polanco, 11510, Mexico DF, MEXICO. Tel: (5) 281 5486. Fax: (5) 281 5212. E-mail: *kiwimexico@compuserve.com.mx*.

New Zealand Embassy, Carnegielaan 10, 2517 KH The Hague, THE NETHERLANDS. Tel: (70) 346 9324. Immigration (70) 365 8037. Fax: (70) 363 2983. Immigration (70) 364 0116.

E-mail: *nzemb@bart.nl*.

New Zealand Consulate, Rua de S. Felix, 13-2, 1200 Lisboa, PORTUGAL. Tel: (1) 350 9690. Fax: (1) 572 004.

New Zealand Embassy, 3rd Floor, Plaza de la Lealtad 2, 28014 Madrid, SPAIN. Tel: (1) 523 0226. Fax: (1) 523 0171.

New Zealand Consulate General, 28A Chemin du Petit-Saconnex, CH-1209 Geneva (PO Box 334, CH-1211 Geneva 19), SWITZERLAND. Tel: (22) 734 9530. Fax: (22) 734 3062. E-mail: *newzeal@pop.unicc.org*.

New Zealand Immigration Service, New Zealand House, Haymarket, London SW1Y 4TQ, UNITED KINGDOM. Tel: 0991 100 100. Fax: (020) 7973 0370.

New Zealand Embassy, 37 Observatory Circle NW, Washington DC 20008, UNITED STATES OF AMERCA. Tel: (202) 328 4800. Fax: (202) 667 5227. E-mail: *nz@nzemb.org*.

New Zealand Consulate General, Suite 1150, 12400 Wilshire Boulevard, Los Angeles, CA 90025, UNITED STATES OF AMERICA. Tel: (310) 207 1605. Fax: (310) 207 3605.

New Zealand High Commission, Eastgate Centre (8th Floor Greenbridge), corner of Robert Mugabe Road and Second Street (PO Box 5448), Harare, ZIMBABWE. Tel: (4) 759 221. Fax: (4) 759 228.

New Zealand Offices

New Zealand Immigration Service, Private Bag, Wellesley Street, Auckland, New Zealand. Tel: 09 914 4100. Fax: 09 914 4119.

New Zealand Immigration Service, 5th Floor Westpac Building, Victoria Street, Private Bag, Hamilton, New Zealand. Tel: 07 838 3566. Fax: 07 838 0059.

New Zealand Immigration Service, Level 7, Regional Council Centre, 142-146 Wakefield Street, PO Box 27-149, Wellington, New Zealand. Tel: 04 384 7929. Fax: 04 384 8243.

New Zealand Immigration Service, Carter House, 81 Lichfield Street, PO Box 22-111, Christchurch, New Zealand. Tel: 03 365 2520. Fax: 03 365 2530. Website: *www.immigration.govt.nz*.

Immigration consultants

Ambler Collins, Eden House, 59 Fulham High Street, London SW6 3JJ. Tel: (020) 7371 0123. E-mail: *amblercollins@compuserve.com*.

EDUCATION

Ministry of Education Offices (Website: *www.minedu.govt.nz*)
National Office, 45–47 Pipitea Street, PO Box 1666, Thorndon, Wellington. Tel: 04 473 5544. Fax: 04 499 1327.

Regional Offices:
39–45 College Hill, Private Bag 47-911, Ponsonby, Auckland 1034. Tel: 09 377 7655. Fax: 09 302 3019.
Corner of Grey and Bridge Streets, Private Bag 3011, Hamilton. Tel: 07 838 3705. Fax: 07 838 3710.
E-mail: *sheila.richmond@minedugovt nz.*
2nd Floor, 65 Waterloo Road, Lower Hutt, Wellington. Tel: 04 566 1219. Fax: 03 364 1631.
Box 2522, Christchurch, New Zealand. Tel: 03 365 7386. Fax (operations): 03 34 1631. Fax (property): 03 364 1667.
PO Box 1225, Dunedin, New Zealand. Tel: 03 474 0152. Fax: 03 479 0250.

Polytechnics
Waikato Polytechnic, Tristram Street, Private Bag 3036, Hamilton. Tel: 07 834 888. Fax: 07 838 0707.
Taranaki Polytechnic, Main Bell Street, New Plymouth. Tel: 06 757 3100. Fax: 06 757 8261. Website: *www.taranaki.ac.nz.*
Central Institute of Technology, PO Box 40-740, Somme Road, Heretaunga, Upper Hutt, Wellington. Tel: 04 914 2000. Fax: 04 914 2089. E-mail: *courseinfo@cit.ac.nz.* Website: *www.cit.ac.nz.*
Christchurch Polytechnic, PO Box 22-095, Coventry Street, Christchurch. Tel: 03 379 8150. Fax: 03 366 6544.
Otago Polytechnic, Forth Street, Private Bag 1910, Dunedin. Tel: 03 477 3014. Fax: 03 477 6032. E-mail: *info@tekotago.ac.nz.* Website: *www.tekotago.ac.nz.*
Southland Institute of Technology, Tay Street, Invercargill. Tel: 03 218 2599. Fax: 04 214 4977. E-mail: *marketing@southpoly.ac.nz.*
Association of Polytechnics, PO Box 10-344, Wellington. Tel: 04 471 1162. Fax: 04 473 2350.

Schools
Kamo Christian College, 55 Great North Road, Whangerei. Tel: 09 435 2458. Fax: 09 435 0458. E-mail: *postmaster@kcc.school.nz.*
Hato Petera College (ages 13–18), 103 College Road, Northcote, Auckland. Tel/Fax: 09 480 7784.

Kirstin School (ages 5–18), 360 Albany Highway, Albany, PO Box 87, Auckland. Tel: 09 415 9566. Fax: 09 415 8495.

Diocesan School for Girls (ages 5–18), Margot Street, Epsom, Auckland. Tel: 09 520 0221. Fax: 09 520 6778.

Collegiate School (ages 5–18), Liverpool Street, Private Bag, Wanganui. Tel: 06 349 0210. Fax: 06 349 0280. E-mail: *wcs@collegiate.school.nz*.

The Correspondence School, 11 Portland Crescent, Private Bag, Wellington. Tel: 04 473 6841. Fax: 04 471 2406.

Colleges of Education

Auckland College of Education, Private Bag 92-601, Symonds Street, Auckland. Tel: 09 623 8899. Fax: 09 623 8898.

University of Waikato, Hill Crest Road, Hamilton. Tel: 07 856 2889.

Massey University College of Education, Private Bag 11-222, Palmerston North. Tel: 06 356 9099. Fax: 06 350 5799.

Wellington College of Education, Donald Street, PO Box 17-310, Karori, Wellington. Tel: 06 476 8699. Fax: 04 476 7189.

Christchurch College of Education, Dovetail Avenue, PO Box 31-065, Christchurch. Tel: 03 348 2059. Fax: 03 348 4311. Website: *www.cce.ac.nz*.

Dunedin College of Education, 145 Union Street East, Private Bag 1912, Dunedin. Tel: 03 477 2289. Fax: 03 477 6573. Website: *www.dce.ac.nz*.

A helpful directory

A *Directory of New Zealand Schools and Tertiary Institutions May 1999* is available at a cost of NZ$30.00 from Learning Media Ltd. PO Box 3293, Wellington, New Zealand. Tel: 04 471 5549. Fax: 04 472 64444. E-mail: *orders@learningmedia.co.nz*.

FOR WOMEN

Rural Women New Zealand, 30 Hawkestone Street, Thorndon, Wellington. Tel: 04 473 5524. Fax: 04 472 8946. E-mail: *ruralwomen@clear.net.nz*. Website: *www.ruralcomen.org*.

Ministry of Women's Affairs, 48 Mulgrave Street, PO Box 10-049, Wellington. Tel: 04 473 4112. Fax: 04 472 0961. E-mail: *mwa@mwa.govt.nz*. Website: *www.mwa.govt.nz*.

MOTORING

Avis Car Rentals
Level 2, Building 4, Central Park 666, Great South Street,
    Auckland. Tel: 09 526 2800. Fax: 09 526 2828.
Christchurch Airport, 76 Orchard Road, Christchurch. Tel: 03 358
    9661. Fax: 03 379 4602.

Hertz Rentals
    Corner of Tory and Buckle Streets, Wellington. Tel: 04 384 3809.
    154 Victoria Street West, Auckland. Tel: 09 367 6350.
    46 Lichfield Street, Christchurch. Tel: 03 366 0549.

AA Automobile Association Inc. Website: *www.nzaa.co.nz*.
    342–352 Lambton Quay, Wellington. Tel: 04 470 9999.
    99 Albert Street, Auckland. Tel: 09 377 4660. Fax: 09 309 4564.
    210 Hereford Street, Christchurch. Tel: 03 379 1280.
    410 Anglesea Street, Hamilton. Tel: 07 839 1397.

Motor Trade Association Inc. 32–34 Kent Terrace, PO Box 9244,
    Courtenay Place, Wellington. Tel: 04 385 8859. Fax: 04 385 9517.
    E-mail: *mta@motor-trade.co.nz*. Website: *www.mta.co.nz*.

PROFESSIONAL AND TRADE ASSOCIATIONS

General

New Zealand Chamber of Commerce UK, 393 The Strand, London,
    WC2. Tel: (020) 7379 0720. Fax: (020) 7379 0721.

Medical

New Zealand Medical Association, PO Box 156, Wellington. Tel: 04
    472 4741. Fax: 04 471 0838. E-mail: *nzma@nzma.org.nz*. Website:
    www.nzma.org.nz.
Pharmaceutical Society of New Zealand, 124 Dixon Street,
    Wellington. Tel: 04 802 0030. Fax: 04 382 9297.
New Zealand Nurses Organisation, 181–183 Willis Street, Well-
    ington. Tel: 04 385 0847. Fax: 04 382 9993.
Pharmacy Guild of New Zealand Inc. National Headquarters,
    Pharmacy House, 124 Dixon Street, Wellington. Tel: 04 385 8200.
New Zealand Association of Optometrists, 49 Boulcott Street,
    Wellington. Tel: 04 473 2322. Fax: 04 473 2328.
Dental Council of NZ, 108 The Terrace, PO Box 10-448, Wellington.

Tel: 04 499 4820.

Researched Medicines Industry Association NZ Inc. Level 8 Castrol House, 36 Custom House Quay, PO Box 10-447, Wellington. Tel: 04 499 4277. Fax: 04 385 9003.

New Zealand Veterinary Association, 69 Boulcott Street, Wellington. Tel: 04 471 0484. Fax: 04 471 0494.

Farming

Deer Farmers Association, Level 10, Lambton Quay, Wellington. Tel: 04 472 5092. Fax: 04 472 5151.

Federated Farmers of NZ Inc. Corner of Featherston and Johnston Streets, Wellington. Tel: 04 473 7269. Fax: 04 473 1081.

Nursery and Garden Industry Association of New Zealand Inc. PO Box 3443, Wellington. Tel: 04 385 3511.

Legal

New Zealand Police Association Inc. 57 Willis Street, Wellington. Tel: 04 472 0198. Fax: 04 471 1309.

New Zealand Law Society, 26 Waring Taylor Street, Wellington. Tel: 04 472 7837. Fax: 04 473 7909.

Technical

Aviation Industry Association of NZ Inc. 12 Johnston Street, Wellington. Tel: 04 472 2707.

Cement & Concrete Association of NZ, Level 16, 142 Featherston Street, PO Box 448, Wellington. Tel: 04 499 8820. Fax: 04 499 7760.

Electrical Contractors Association of New Zealand Inc. Corner of Vivian and Marion Streets, Wellington. Tel: 04 385 9657. Fax: 04 385 4645.

HANZ (Hospitality Association of New Zealand), 178 Willis Street, Wellington. Tel: 04 385 1369. Fax: 04 384 8044.

Institute of Environmental Science & Research, PO Box 12-444, Wellington. Tel: 04 237 0149. Fax: 04 237 2369.

Institute of Geological & Nuclear Sciences Limited (GNS), PO Box 30-368, Lower Hutt, Wellington. Tel: 04 570 1444. Fax: 04 570 4600. Website: *www.gns.cri.nz*.

Institute of Professional Engineers New Zealand, PO Box 12-241, Thorndon, Wellington. Tel: 04 473 9444. Fax: 04 473 2324. Website: *www.ipenz.org.nz*.

ITANZ (Information Technology Association of New Zealand Inc), 9th Floor, 108 The Terrace, PO Box 1710, Wellington. Tel: 04 472

2731. Fax: 04 499 3318. E-mail: *info@itanz.org.nz*. Website: *www.itanz.org.nz*.

New Zealand Architects Co-op Society, 69 Rutherford Street, Lower Hutt, Wellington. Tel: 04 566 4762.

New Zealand Chemical Industry Council, 12 Johnston Street, Wellington. Tel: 04 499 4311. Fax: 04 472 7100.

New Zealand Computer Society, Paxus House, 73 Boulcott Street, Wellington. Tel: 04 473 1043. Fax: 04 473 1025.

New Zealand Painting Contractors Association (Inc), 63 Miramar Avenue, Miramar, Wellington. Tel: 04 388 1516.

Printing Industries NZ, Huddart Parker Building, Post Office Square, Wellington. Tel: 04 472 3497. Fax: 04 472 3534.

Retail Merchants Association, PO Box 13-877, Christchurch. Tel: 03 366 1308.

New Zealand Timber Industry Federation Inc, 2 Maginnity Street, Wellington. Tel: 04 473 5200.

Wellington Master Plumbers Association, 108 Taranaki Street, PO Box 6606, Wellington. Tel: 04 384 4184. Fax: 04 384 2456.

Employers and Manufacturers Association (Central) Inc, 95-99 Molesworth Street, Wellington. Tel: 04 473 7224. Fax: 04 473 4501.

Financial

New Zealand Bankers Association, Level 12 Grand Arcade Tower, 16 Willis Street, Wellington. Tel: 04 472 8838. Fax: 04 473 1698. E-mail: *acopland@nzba.org.nz*.

Institute of Chartered Accountants, Cigna House, 40 Mercer Street, PO Box 11-342, Manners Street, Wellington. Tel: 04 474 7840. Fax: 04 473 6303. Website: *www.icanz.co.nz*.

Education

New Zealand Post Primary Teachers Association (PPTA), 1 Edward Street, Wellington. Tel: 04 384 9964.

Further Reading

TRAVEL GUIDES

Beautiful New Zealand, Peter Morath (Hale, 1993).
Christchurch: A City and its People, Philip Temple (Pacific, 1987).
Collins Illustrated Guide to New Zealand, Elizabeth Booz (Collins, 1989).
Cycle Touring in Neu Zealand, J. B. Ringer (Mountaineer Books, USA, 1989).
Fragile Eden: A Ride Through New Zealand, Robin Hanbury-Tenison (Arrow, 1990).
Guide to Auckland, Brigid Pike (Hodder & Stoughton, 1987).
Homeplaces: Three Coasts of the South Island of New Zealand, Keri Hulme (Hodder & Stoughton, 1989).
Insider's Guide to New Zealand, Kirsten Ellis (Moorland, 1993).
Insight Guides: New Zealand (APA Publications, Hong Kong, 1992).
Introduction to New Zealand, Elizabeth Booz (The Guide Book Co, Hong Kong, 1991).
Mobile New Zealand Travel Guide, D. & J. Pope, two vols (North Island and South Island) (Heinemann Reed, 1992).
New Zealand in Your Pocket, Arnold Schuchter (Horizon, 1990).
New Zealand 1993 (Fodor Gold Guides, 1993).
New Zealand Travel Survival Kit, Tony Wheeler (Lonely Planet, 1991).
New Zealand, Gift of the Sea, Brian Brake (Hodder & Stoughton, 1990).
West Coast Pictorial, John Burford (Whitcoulls, 1987).
Wild New Zealand (Reader's Digest Australia, 1993).

FOOD AND WINE

Jane MacQuitty's Pocket Guide to Australian and New Zealand Wines, Jane MacQuitty (Mitchell Beazley, 1990).
New Zealand, the Beautiful Cookbook, Tui Flower (Weldon

Australia, 1992).
New Zealand Food and How To Cook It, David Burford (Bateman, New Zealand, 1992).

SPORT AND LEISURE

Between the Posts: A New Zealand Rugby Anthology, Ron Palenski (Hodder & Stoughton, 1989).
Fishing the Wild Places of New Zealand, Tony Orman (Bush Press. New Zealand, 1991).
Golf Courses of South Canterbury, Peter Russell (Whitcoulls, 1985).
Golf Courses of Wellington, Peter Russell (Whitcoulls, 1985).

NATURAL HISTORY

Dragonflies of New Zealand, Richard Rowe (Auckland University Press, 1987).
Ferns of New Zealand, Susan Firth (Hodder & Stoughton, 1986).
Field Guide to the Birds of New Zealand, R. Falla (Collins, 1979).
Handbook of New Zealand Mammals, Carolyn King (Oxford University Press, 1990).
Living New Zealand Forest, Robert Brockie (Bateman, New Zealand, 1992).

EDUCATION

Family, School and Community, Peter Ramsay (Allen & Unwin, 1984).
The New Zealand Education Directory (annual), available from Consyl Publishing, 3 Buckhurst Road, Bexhill-on-Sea, TN40 IQF.
Towards Successful Schooling: Conference Proceedings, Hugh Lauder & Cathy Wylie (Falmer, 1990).

BUSINESS & LAW

Business Review Monthly Newspaper, available from Consyl Publishing, 3 Buckhurst Road, Bexhill-on-Sea TN40 IQF.
Corporatization and Privatization: Lessons from New Zealand, Ian Duncan & Alan Bollard (Oxford University Press, 1993).

Economic History of New Zealand, M. F. L. Prichard (Collins, 1970).

Fair Trading in New Zealand, B. Hill & M. Jones (Butterworth NZ, 1989).

Family Law Policy in New Zealand, Frank Henaghan & W. Atkin (Oxford University Press, 1993).

Introduction to Financial Markets in New Zealand, G. Karacaoglu (Victoria University Press, 1988).

Introduction to the New Zealand Legal System, R. D. Mulholland (Butterworth NZ, 1990).

The New Zealand Economy: A Personal View, Robert Muldoon (Endeavour NZ, 1985).

Takeover New Zealand, W. B. Sutch (Reed, 1972).

Towards Prosperity, Roger Douglas (Bateman NZ, 1991).

Turning it Around: Closure and Revitalization in New Zealand Industry, John Savage & Alan Bollard (Oxford University Press, 1991).

HISTORY

Forever the Forest: A West Coast Story, Neville Peat (Hodder & Stoughton, 1987).

Fifth Wind: New Zealand and the Legacy of a Turbulent Past, Robert MacDonald (Bloomsbury, 1989).

Historic Places of New Zealand, Automobile Association/Historic Places Trust (Hodder & Stoughton, 1981).

History of New Zealand, Keith Sinclair (Penguin, 1989).

Hokianga, Jack Lee (Hodder & Stoughton, 1987).

Maori Magna Carta: New Zealand Law and the Treaty of Waitangi, Paul McHugh (Oxford University Press, 1992).

Ka Whawhai Tonu Matou: Struggle Without End, Ranginui Walker (Penguin, 1990).

New Zealand: A Short History, Laurie Barber (Hutchinson, 1990).

Oxford Illustrated History of New Zealand, Keith Sinclair (Oxford University Press, 1990).

The Past Today: Historic Places in New Zealand, John Wilson (New Zealand Historic Places Trust/Pacific, 1987).

Oxford History of New Zealand, W. Oliver & B. Williams (Oxford University Press, 1993).

GOVERNMENT AND POLITICS

Democracy and Power in New Zealand, Richard Mulgan (Oxford University Press, 1989).

The Ideal Society and its Enemies: The Foundations of Modern New Zealand Society, Miles Fairburn (Auckland University Press, 1989).

Justice, Ethics and New Zealand Society, Graham Oddies & R. Perrett (Oxford University Press, 1993).

Local and Regional Government in New Zealand, Claudia Scott (Allen & Unwin, 1979).

Maori: The Crisis and the Challenge, Alan Duff (HarperCollins 1993).

New Zealand in Crisis, D. Novits & B. Willmot (GP Publications, 1992).

New Zealand Foreign Affairs Handbook, Steve Hoadley (Oxford University Press, 1993).

Nuclear Free the New Zealand Way, David Lange (Penguin, 1990).

Politics in New Zealand: A Reader, Steven Pevine (Allen & Unwin, 1978).

Unbridled Power: An Interpretation of New Zealand's Constitution and Government, Geoffrey Palmer (Oxford University Press, 1987).

Women's Suffrage in New Zealand, Patricia Grimshaw (Auckland University Press, 1988).

LITERATURE, MUSIC AND ART

Anthology of Twentieth Century New Zealand Poetry, Vincent O'Sullivan (Oxford University Press, 1987).

Goodbye to Romance: Stories by New Zealand and Australian Women Writers 1930-88, E. Webby & L. Wevers (Unwin, 1990).

History of New Zealand Music, John Masefield Thompson (Oxford University Press, 1991).

Introduction to New Zealand Painting 1839-1980, Gordon Brown (Bateman, NZ, 1992).

Oxford History of New Zealand Literature in English, Terry Sturm (Oxford University Press, 1992).

Penguin Book of Contemporary New Zealand Poetry, Miriam Evans (Penguin, 1990).

Two Hundred Years of New Zealand Paintings, Gil Docking (Bateman, NZ, 1992).

Index